GRATITUDE
Always...

A Woman's Journey to Total Trust in Spirit

D E B O R A H   L I N D H O L M

Foundation for Women
Post Office Box 2786
La Jolla, CA 92038

858-483-0400
1-888-303-2622
www.foundationforwomen.org

Cover illustration and internal illustrations by Jane Ellen Davis
www.unlockyourheart.com
Book design and pagination by Tommy Gaebel
www.tommygaebel.com

First Edition
ISBN-13: 9781502741158

This Book

This book, the title, and the front cover all came to me – I did not go looking for any of it, never wanted to write a book, never wanted the world to know my personal story.

I started writing and the messages came – quickly with ease and grace – and kept coming.

One morning just as I was about to awake, I saw the cover of the book – the purple, the heart and the words on the front are the image I saw that early morning. I drew them and wrote them immediately – and they have not changed. It is not my design.

I also knew there was only one artist who could be involved in this project and she is; thank you dearest Janie.

Gratitude always.

Contents

Chapter 1

The Journey

Gratitude

I was touched deeply years ago by Victor Frankl's *"Man's Search for Meaning"* where he notes that despite one's circumstances, one always has a choice to choose one's attitude. Gratitude always?

Sitting alone by the sea this morning, I feel it, gratitude.

Can I reframe everything and hold it all with gratitude?

Is every experience in my life contributing to the evolution of my soul?

Is everything happening just as it needs to for my highest good and enlightenment?

Can I be sobbing with sadness and filled with gratitude at the same time?

Years ago one of my meditation teachers shared a special practice during a retreat. Imagine that everyone on the planet is enlightened except you – and that everyone is doing exactly what they need to be doing so that you will become enlightened. What a powerful practice. And part of how I have come to choose gratitude always. Despite my circumstances I do have a choice. I can bemoan the experience or thank God and all Angels helping me with another important lesson.

Just how many more are there? I told my spiritual teacher Verniece years ago that I am at the plate and will not walk away – keep the lessons coming. I have tried to renegotiate that commitment a few times but only for brief moments. I am filled with gratitude always for each and every lesson.

"Be who you are and do what you came for"

Thanks to one of our treasured supporters of the Foundation for Women, Robin, a dear and powerful book landed in my lap, *"Save the World and Still Be Home for Dinner."*

I devour books, am constantly absorbed in: *"Gandhi"* or *"The Price of Inequity"* or *"Women, Spirituality and Transformative Leadership"* or *"Great by Choice"* or *"Happiness is an Inside Job"* or *"The Soul of Money"* or *"Half the Sky"* or *"The Gift"* and *"I Heard God Laughing"* or…

Robin's sharing of her new favorite book is a gift from you Divine Mother and the timing is astonishing. Since I returned from a spiritual adventure to Peru the end of 2012, the months of 2013 and 2014 have been filled with one major loss after another. I have been feeling like a baseball bat has continually been striking me below the knees – getting me on my knees – which apparently is where I have needed to be.

Much like my experience, the author of *"Save the World and Still Be Home for Dinner"* felt like he was being continually hit by a truck, one right after another, at one point in his life. The book's message and wisdom has so helped to lift the fog, helped me realize the losses were necessary. It also has restored my energy, diminished the grief and renewed my commitment to the work of the Foundation for Women at an even greater level. It has helped me realize how important it is to be who you are and do what you came for.

I am beyond grateful to know that and beyond grateful to you, Robin, for the lifeline out of the soup. So grateful…

Bricks in my Foundation

When speaking of the work of the Foundation for Women, I often say that God had a very good idea and I was blessed to hear it. It is so much bigger than me. I get that.

When the "knowing" to create the Foundation for Women came to me, I drew a foundation full of bricks, something that would hold up a structure of some sort. Instead the foundation has held up women, given them strength, a sense of community, courage and hope.

As the Foundation for Women began developing, I began exploring the bricks in my personal foundation. There were so many bricks that felt icky to me, so many experiences I wanted to push away, so much hurt and pain.

After a life time of hurry, fix it, make it better there was not one single person on the planet who knew my entire story. I had come to believe that healing comes from saying something out loud to God, myself and another human being. So the Universe brought dear friend Jack into my life. As Pat Brown had truly seen me when I was a teenager, Jack saw me then when I was in my 40's as an adult. He was curious. He listened. He asked questions. He didn't turn away from the icky. He helped me realize that all the bricks in my foundation are needed for me to be solid today; push some away or remove some and I would not be able to stand firmly on this planet and do the important and continually emerging work.

It was not an easy process telling my story to another human being. I sobbed with deep, deep sadness. But for the first time I started to understand that I needed all of it, that I could surround it all with loving-kindness and compassion as had become my practice for all beings, except for me. I added the words "including me" into my daily prayer. "I offer this prayer of love and compassion, dedicating all of my actions this day to the benefit of all living beings, including me." I noticed the pushing away and reframed the pattern with compassion, something I still continue to do.

Jack is forever on my gratitude list.

Being Quiet with Me

I am alone sitting in a one-bedroom apartment in Bangkok. Wherever my eyes land there is beauty and peace from the large vase of lucky bamboo to the beautiful Thai tapestries on the bed. And I am being quiet with me.

It is Monday afternoon here. Everyone in California is just going to bed, ending their Sunday as I am well into my Monday. I am committing to several hours of quiet with me and some writing.

Being quiet with me has not always been easy. Somehow I needed to do instead of be so much of this life. Giving myself permission to be quiet this afternoon instead of visiting one more place or staying in conversation over yet another meal with my traveling companions or… I am noticing what is arising. To my surprise it is more peace than angst, more gratitude than desire to do. Joy – this moment of quiet when outside my door more than 10 million people are busy doing.

I am so very grateful for this moment.

Epiphanies

They come without my invitation. They jolt me unsteady. They get my attention. I pay attention.

"This is not about anyone else's behavior – this is about your behavior, Deborah!"

Yikes! I awoke to this knowing one Friday morning – from where?? I sat with it. Meditated with it. Had tea with it. Became friends with it. And sure enough – embraced it as the truth.

I have spent my life trying to make people feel, think and do things they don't want to feel, think and do. And I have driven them and myself crazy in the process. As many times as I need to be reminded, it is all about my side of the sidewalk – only about my behavior.

Since I started the Foundation for Women, I wanted everyone who found their way to us to be as passionate as I am about ending poverty, about being the voice for those who are not heard, to commit their philanthropic and emotional energy to this support of more than half our human family. So many came – and over the years so many have left. I am powerless over other people and their behavior, and yet I am continually surprised.

I guess I have not learned the lesson yet. But I am committed to doing so.

In *"The Mastery of Love"* Don Miguel Ruiz talks of the two tracks of love and fear, and that most of humanity operates from the track of fear. That track tries to control others, has expectations, wants desired outcomes. I have never thought of myself as a person coming from fear – but am I behaving like that?

Bam – back to the fact that it is all about my behavior and not anyone else's. It is not about those who have come and gone. Or those who don't support. Or those who think only of their neighborhood instead of our global family. Or those who have a job instead of a passion. My focus is not on others – it is only on me and my behavior.

Epiphanies, deep spiritual knowings, keep coming as spiritual reminders to keep the focus on my side of the sidewalk. I can be present with and change my behavior only. I am powerless over others and their behavior. I am grateful for epiphanies.

Expectations

I find myself with them often. And I set myself up for resentment and disappointment when my hopes and wishes don't happen.

I am about to take the first two-week vacation since I started the Foundation for Women nearly 20 years ago. I am going to a yoga retreat in the UK with Swami Veda, and will spend a few days in London with dear friends and then a week-long walking adventure in the Lake District of England with David Whyte.

I am tired and weary and so ready for this marvelous time out and adventure – so full of expectations for a life-impacting experience.

And I am reminded about a conversation years ago. After an early morning dance class before the Foundation for Women was birthed, I exclaimed to fellow dancer Devon that I was going on this yoga retreat in Northern California and it was going to be the best thing that ever happened to me!

She listened quietly and attentively and finally said, "Do you think you can go without any expectations Deborah??"

WOW – what a concept!

That inquiry is such an anchor in mindfulness and present moment thinking for me. I have my expectations and I have a tool to bring me back – when I remember to use it…

I am grateful.

Sobbing with Sadness

Two months of non-stop work with my dearest sister Emily, first in Liberia and then in the US and in Canada, are complete. I am in my sacred sanctuary by the sea alone, exhausted.

I am looking forward to Tuesday Night Date Night with a dear friend. He had promised that he would clear his calendar this week; that once Emily was on the plane home to Liberia we would have a quiet week.

Expectations = preconceived resentment. How long I have known this and yet once again my expectation has led to resentment.

He did not honor Tuesday Night Date Night. I am sobbing with exhaustion and sadness. He is the most recent in a lifetime of people who are not available; one after another after another I bring them to me.

Can my sobbing with sadness finally shift to gratitude?

Am I finally getting this huge life lesson? I cannot make unavailable people available. Instead of disappointment, is he my greatest teacher to help me finally get this lesson? Gratitude always.

Can I turn to gratitude for everything?

Stages of Grief

It is not the first time we have separated – but it is the last. I so know that. So here I am face to face with grief, a process I know well from years of hospice work, but now I am intimately being with it instead of just knowing it.

When he showed up in my life totally unexpectedly years ago, there was an energy and deep knowing that I had never experienced. I wasn't surprised when Verniece said, "You have been waiting for this your whole life." I knew something was very different. He was my life partner. After all my hurry, fix it, make it better experiences, my life partner had arrived.

Rotary brought us together – a commitment to and love of service. Our minds, both brilliant, worked the same. And our hearts, big and generous, matched. Unexpected joy when I was in my 50's and totally content being single and growing the Foundation for Women – surprise!

And then slowly it began – the downward spiral. We separated several times but the Universe always put us back together. There was more learning and loving to do, better together than apart. Until alcohol and food could no longer fill the huge hole. So he turned to sex and wanted to take monogamy off the table. The end. It turns out he had already taken monogamy off the table so was trying to clear his conscious after the fact. Yikes! Really? Unbelievably sad.

Deep rage sent him and a night intruder one evening both out of my life forever – along with everyone else who had ever been abusive to me or my work. The power I found in my tremendous scream and fury gave me strength – and still does. But disbelief and sadness and loneliness have now joined that initial rage.

The journey of untreated addictions is clearly visible.

A colleague reminded me this week that my former lover, partner and best friend is sacred and holy and that his soul is doing exactly what needs to be done for his highest good and learning. I can intellectually accept and embrace that and find some comfort. But the loss remains the reality.

I am grateful for all the joy and learning the last years brought – and grateful to know that the stages of grief are just that, stages, and that today is not a destination; there is acceptance on the other side of this loss. Gratitude always sustains me.

Am I Finished???

"You're finished when the dirt covers you," said Verniece. Once I saw how it all fit together – unavailable partners, hurry, fix it, make it better behavior, finding my life work and purpose – it all seemed "finished"…

Just a month later I sat with Verniece and laughed at my speculation! No I am not done. And now I have a tiger by the tail.

I love the images. I don't fit as I am living above water and most of the world is living below water. One is not better than the other, just different. All good. Now the image of a tiger and my job is just to hang on. Verniece gets tired looking at my life right now – so much! And then offers peace to the discussion: the tiger is G-O-D. Yikes!

I have been surrendering to God, Mother Earth, all Buddhas, all Enlightened Ones daily for more than 30 years. Could it be that I truly am doing God's work and that I am being guided as I request every day as well? Could it just be my job to keep holding onto that tail?

I am a long way from being finished. Gratitude always…

Chapter 2

Not Fitting

Verniece

I found my way to a special healer when I was in my 40's – after reading more books and doing more therapy and keeping more journals and sitting in more meditation retreats and doing more yoga than I thought possible. For years I would make my way to her beachfront haven almost an hour south of where I live every other Friday afternoon. Verniece became my link to sanity.

I never fit. A massage therapist once told me that I am "a turtle born into a world of rabbits." Another learning. It so made sense to me. But what to do with that information?

Verniece and I are very connected. I refer to her as my spiritual signpost. When I want to go away, she grounds me on this planet. I chose to come she reminds me; really?

After many years of working together, I "knew" one New Year's Eve day that when we finished our session it was time for me to try to stand on my own. I stopped my regular treks to the south. I filled my Friday afternoons in other ways. I thought I could go it alone. Wrong.

After two years, I returned from yet another long trip to Africa and "knew" I had to call her. I had to see her. She came to me. We hugged as if no time had elapsed. She listened. She knew. "You don't fit Deborah," she said. Such relief at the acknowledgment. She knew what I felt deeply. Now what?

She showed me the pattern. My father had made me his psychological and emotional partner as my mother was not available. He loved me – but he was not available. The pattern began as a very small girl.

Love = connecting with unavailable people.

Even though as an adult I told my father to stop calling me, that I could not be his partner, I did not know there was a pattern. Not until it happened again and again and again…

I am in my sixties and I now know the pattern. A life-time of sadness, of trying to make unavailable people available. Exhausting. And I am continuing to work with Verniece. There is always more to do.

I said to Verniece once, "I am at the plate. Please keep the lessons coming. I don't want to waste a minute of this precious lifetime." I am committed. And I am so grateful.

Texting with the VP

I have a very dear friend – the Vice President of Liberia. We met during my first trip to Liberia in December 2006 and my life has been blessed by his presence and our connection ever since.

I have often had the feeling this life time that I did not fit; in fact more often than not. I somehow arrived into a biological family where I did not fit – really I am supposed to be here? I don't think people are supposed to act this way? What about kindness and compassion and being nice to one another?

I spent my childhood as a bystander, watching and feeling like I was from some other world. I was always taller than others. I loved solitude and contemplation instead of family dinners. I longed for a mother who loved and cared about me. I ached for a sense of connection.

I spent much of my adult years trying to hurry, fix it, make it better when I felt like I did not fit. I changed relationships and connections that did not sustain a sense of belonging.

Now I know it was all part of the plan; all part of what I agreed to do this lifetime. I signed up to come into this life without my tribe. I volunteered to be the white woman in America who could bridge the gap between different worlds. I volunteered to be the voice for those whose voices are not heard. I volunteered to be of service to others who do not fit in.

The work of the Foundation for Women and particularly the work in Liberia have reconnected me to my tribe. I am at home as I have never been before. I am surrounded by people I love and treasure, and who love and treasure me. I feel it in my heart and bones. And I am blessed to be of service to many.

Spiritual Sanctuary

I am so blessed with a sacred space next to the ocean. I thank God every day and continually wonder "How did a young girl from Geneva, Illinois end up here by the sea?"

When I was in my 50s, I started musing about living in a house. Never having had that experience, I started exploring what that might be like. After all, that is what gown-up people do – they have a house and a family and… Not my experience. I had looked at houses and families my entire life – what goes on in there? How are they living?

Despite my knowing that I cannot compare my insides to someone else's out-sides, I longed for that sense of stability, grown-up-ness. So a house appeared – a big house. Four bedrooms, three bathrooms, two decks, 100 acres of open space canyon off the back garden – and a long away view of the sea…

The Vice President of Liberia and his staff were my first guests. They loved the house. Then others came – and came – and came… One night I hosted a delegation (via the US State Department) of a dozen Muslim women from the United Kingdom and four attorneys from Liberia as well as several members of the Foundation for Women. A mini UN in my home – so fabulous!

And then they all left as the others had. And there I was – me alone in a big house. Not what I had imagined for so many years. I had an alarm system for a roommate instead of a family.

While on this house adventure, I had rented and tried to sell my sanctuary by the sea. But it would not let go of me – no matter how hard I tried to "know" that I was now a grown up living in a house.

I am back in my sanctuary by the sea – 1200 square feet of heaven on this earth – and only by divine guidance. I am so grateful.

Star light, star bright,

first star I see tonight…

I wish I may,

I wish I might,

Have this wish I wish tonight: "Please get me out of here!"

That was my continual wish as a child every night. I knew I had landed in the wrong place, the wrong family, the wrong everything.

Staring just now out the east facing vaulted ceiling windows of my special sanctuary by the sea, I see the most brilliant first star of the night – and that childhood wish comes back to me instantly. "Please get me out of here" has now been replaced with "Please may all I do be for the highest good of all beings."

Childhood pain and agony transformed to service.

And a huge wonderment – how many young girls are saying the equivalent of my "Star light, star bright" request this moment all over the planet? How many are in circumstances beyond my imagination and comprehension?

I am connected to them all – and committed to them all – and beyond grateful for this childhood pleading which has turned into service to others.

May a multitude of beings benefit from this life-time commitment to service… Gratitude always.

It's a God thing...

I grew up in a small community in the middle of the US with 10,000 people and cornfields. As a small child I used to talk to God each evening from my bedroom window. "Star light, star bright, first star I see tonight, I wish I may, I wish I might – please get me out of here!" I knew I did not fit.

I did not get out for years and years. I stopped asking God. I stopped believing.

Now I look at everything and think "It's a God thing…" I certainly could not have survived this life time without God and the band of Angels around me. How did that young girl who landed as an alien in the small community of Geneva, Illinois end up a global citizen doing global work?? It's a God thing…

I believe and I am so grateful.

A Conversation with my Parents

Out of the blue it happened – a Sunday afternoon when I called to check in just to say hello – the greatest conversation with my parents of my life happened, all by apparent accident. Divine Mother thank you!

A beautiful African woman from Ghana has brought them back to their home of 12+ years after months of hospitals and transitional care. Her name is Georgina. She is the key to them being able to return home as she will now be with them 24/7.

They both spoke of poverty – their own histories with it; the challenges of losing their fathers as children; how little things were such big things when there was so little. They each shared their lives with me in an intimate way they never had previously.

And they shared their gratitude for each other, for their lives, for their blessings, for being able to return to their home thanks to Georgina. I never thought I ever fit in the Lindholm family; thought my being there was truly an accident. I had a deep knowing as a small child that people were supposed to be kind to each other, to support each other, to be of service to each other – not to be continually overwhelmed and scared and angry and controlling.

But maybe it was all not an accident. Maybe seeds of gratitude always were planted in me from them at a very early age – and now I am able to see the results of that gift.

It was an unexpected and beyond dear conversation; a miracle actually. I am so grateful.

Chapter 3

The Meaning of Things

Heart Energy

I have hearts everywhere. Glass hearts, stone hearts, wooden hearts. Hearts that hold candles. Hearts from Africa, hearts from my home community of La Jolla. Big hearts, little hearts. Red hearts, purple hearts, blue hearts. Small hearts I can squeeze in my palm and big hearts that are works of art and decorate my sacred sanctuary. I love them all.

I have a favorite – a small crystal-clear heart that has been shattered but remains together in one piece. The lines of breakage fill the heart. Yet somehow it has survived. It is the symbol of my heart. It is beautiful. It gives me hope.

Gratitude is heart energy. It does not come from the head.

There is a special loving-kindness meditation that has been part of my practice for years and years. It comes from a loving heart and is a 2500+-year-old practice used to open loving-kindness and friendliness to oneself and others. The practice is to begin with oneself because without loving oneself it is impossible to love others:

May I be free of worry and fear

May I be peaceful

May I be filled with a sense of well-being

May I be surrounded by loving-kindness and compassion

After directing this meditation to one's self, the practice continues by holding in one's heart and naming benefactors and friends – then people everywhere – and eventually all beings and all living things.

Having this heart energy extend from me to all beings everywhere always gives me great gratitude and joy.

My Rocks

I collect rocks; rocks with meaning.

One of the first rocks that screamed "Take me home with you please!" is a very special flat gray rock inscribed MY RELIGION IS KINDNESS – DALAI LAMA. It came from my favorite florist in La Jolla, Adelaide's, where I have been adopting fabulous orchids for more than 30 years now. I love this rock. I see it every morning when I turn on a small lamp on my altar in the kitchen – and every night when I turn the light out. It speaks to me about so much – how much kindness needs to be a part of every religion and how kindness truly is my religion.

Another rock sits on my kitchen counter next to several photos of African friends. It says simply NURTURE. My dear friend Susan gave it to me when we met in Cambridge several years ago. I am sure she intended for it to be a reminder for me to nurture me as well as others. I am grateful for the reminder. Its bigger meaning for me is to nurture the world – nurture my dear human family, all living creatures and this amazing Mother Earth.

There are two rocks sitting in front of the first Buddha who ever invited me to bring it home from Asia. Simple white rocks, one with the OM symbol and the other with the symbol for and word COMPASSION. I love these rocks. They fit in my palms at the same time and feel so good. The OM rock broke once but glue holds it together now and that seems just fine.

I have a beautifully framed photo of His Holiness the Dalai Lama in my kitchen looking out to the sea. In front of it is my biggest and heaviest rock. It says BLESSINGS in a beautiful script. I have so many blessings.

My favorite framed photo in my sacred sanctuary by the sea is a 5x7" of Emily Guegbeh Peal and me. I love this photo. Emily is my dearest sister. She lives in Liberia and I live in La Jolla and we are connected like no two other sisters. I have two tocks in front of the photo – first a large one that says TRUST GOD and then a small clear one that says THANK YOU.

I have a small blue-grey rock – my Gratitude rock. I hold it often. I look at it often. It rests next to my book of daily Buddhist meditation thoughts. Gratitude always.

My Library

I just went looking for a book in my library – and could not find it. What I did find is the journey of this life time.

I love to read. I devour books. I always have at least a dozen different books right next to my bed. I need books – books about mediation and compassion and love and kindness and life…

This spiritual journey began decades ago and continues. Friend Jan took me into my first metaphysical bookstore in San Diego decades ago – and I bought two books which changed my life completely. John Bradshaw's book *"The Family"* gave me hope that there might be other people on this planet who had some of the same feelings I had. And Melody Beattie's book *"Codependent No More"* enlightened me to the fact that it is impossible for me to change others' behavior; my job is to keep my focus on me.

I did not find the book I was looking for until some time had passed, enough time for me to do a review of the last 30 years. WOW what a journey! And I have not arrived at a destination yet. That realization is in one way exhausting and in another way exhilarating.

I am grateful for every speck of wisdom all those special books contain, and all the wisdom I have yet to read. May it all contribute to my personal growth and well-being and hence benefit all beings.

"It is not easy to find happiness in ourselves, and it is not possible to find it elsewhere." Agnes Repplier

I am so grateful for my library.

My Black Tahitian Pearl Ring

I have very little jewelry. If I don't wear it regularly I don't need to have it. I don't keep special keepsakes in a safe deposit box. I have sold pieces that were part of now closed chapters in my life.

I do have one treasure – my black Tahitian pearl ring which I wear on my right hand always. It does not come off when I shower or when I go the gym.

It was a gift from the Universe when I turned 50. It is substantial in size and was designed by a dear jeweler in my home community La Jolla. It is one of a kind – just like I am one of a kind.

It has become the symbol of my life this journey. It is the only thing I am aware of in nature that grows and becomes more fabulous because of irritation and pain. The more the sand irritates the oyster, the bigger the pearl grows, the more beauty is created. The more challenges I experience, the more trust and love is created in my life.

I need reminders that something bigger is going on, that I am not in charge, that there is always beauty in everything. I treasure this ring for that reason – and am so very grateful for the constant reminder.

Gratitude always.

Joyce

Joyce moved in with me today. She makes me smile!

She is 42 inches high, orange-ish in color and wearing a red hat. She is dressed in a bright yellow mini-skirt and halter top with red and green and white and black accents. Her ballerina slippers are black and white and she has beaded bangles on her wrists and upper arms and around her neck. She is a beyond fabulous doll made in South Africa.

And now I know why she is with me – JOY(ce)! I so love her and her spirit! A dear and special gift of joy from you Divine Mother – so realize that! I can "ce joy" in Joyce!

So grateful…

Dear Doll Emily

She is beautiful. Red hair and a bright smile. Her body is a patch work of experiences and scraps. The result all together is a work of art – a beautiful work of joy – Emily.

I knew her name the moment I saw her more than a decade ago – Emily – and I have no idea why. Artist and friend Sally was having an opening in her gallery one evening; I went; Emily and I bonded immediately and she came home with me that evening.

We have been through a lot during the last 15+ years. She came to my spiritual sanctuary by the sea and settled in wonderfully. Then because of my need for hurry, fix it, make it better, she moved with me to a big house on a big hill. I thought I was creating a family home for my then partner and me. She came with me and patiently waited for attention in an upper story guest room with little acknowledgment for more than three years.

When I came to my senses – a big house does not a family make – and moved back to my spiritual sanctuary by the sea, Emily came as well. But her colorful patchwork and red hair did not fit in the newly renovated space – hardwood floors and Pottery Barn designer furnishings – so she waited patiently again for attention, this time inside a wicker trunk.

This morning many years later as I sat with tea in my now special healing cottage, I reached for Emily and held her close. We rocked in a treasured antique rocking chair. And I cried for the little girl – my little girl – who never felt love, who pushed through every painful experience, who was never held, who made it be okay when it was not okay…

Emily and I are now spending time together regularly – rocking and healing – and sending joy beyond this special healing cottage, ripples to all beings…

Hugs of gratitude…

Giraffes

I am looking at a small, carved wooden giraffe I have had with me since one of the first retreats offered by the Foundation for Women. Several of us went to Santa Fe to spend days with gifted Toltec teacher Maud. It was all beyond amazing – from a sweat lodge to caves to hikes to circles.

At the end of the retreat, Maud guided us to find our power animal, the spirit of the animal world that most spoke to each one of us. My meditation was so clear.

Until that mediation, dear friend Jane would often ask me to swim with her at La Jolla Cove. I made a few brave attempts but my soul and body could not embrace the idea of swimming in such a big pond or the temperature of the water (I love swimming and do it strongly but in 80 degree water in a pool where I can see both sides!). At the end of the meditation it was clear: Jane is octopus and I am a giraffe! Jane and I nodded with love in acknowledgment to each other. She has never asked me to swim with her again; I have never been swimming in the sea since then; giraffes don't swim.

The giraffe connection has continued – in my very frequent travels to Africa and in my home and in my deep knowing. I am continually reaching for God while having my feet on this planet, trying to be in both places at the same time, and doing the best I can.

I love you Maud and Jane and this valuable learning which has been a part of me since that time in Santa Fe – very grateful!

The small giraffe that was made in South Africa is in front of me now; it came home from that retreat with me, given to me by dear friend Barbara, our first FFW board chair.

I am so grateful for this and all the giraffe energy in my life.

My Begging Bowl

On my 48th birthday I was given a very special book with an inscription carefully written inside the front cover:

"There are seasons in human affairs, of inward and outward revolution, when new depths seem to be broken up in the soul, when new wants are unfolded into multitude, and a new undefined good is thirsted for. These are the periods when to dare is the highest wisdom." The author was noted as William E Channing, 1829.

The inscription then ended with *"Happy Birthday Deborah, continue to dare."*

The book, *"Everyday Sacred, a Woman's Journey Home"*, continues to jump off the shelf into my hands. Sue Bender begins the introduction of her book with the words *"This story is about a bowl."*

Today I am reading it yet again and once again reminded of the image of the monk's begging bowl. The monk begins each day with an empty bowl in his hands. Whatever is placed in the bowl will be the nourishment for the day. The practice is to accept everything that is placed in the bowl and be grateful for it.

I love that image. I want to start every day with an empty bowl and trust that whatever lands in it is my nourishment for the day, is exactly what I need. I want to be grateful every day for whatever lands in my bowl.

Some days are easier than others to choose gratitude always. That is why it is called a practice. And that is why every new day begins with an empty bowl.

Chapter 4

Bad Things Happen to Good People

Bad Things Happen to Good People

Bad things do indeed happen to good people. I remember reading the special book of that title by Rabbi Kushner years ago. I am in the soup, again.

To my great surprise after more than 15 years of birthing and running the Foundation for Women, I find myself in wonderment about what has happened in the past few months. How did this organization I birthed lose its core values, its circle model of leadership and its financial stability? Months ago our volunteer and acting COO pointed a finger at me in a meeting and exclaimed, *"You live in a place of optimism called denial Deborah!"* I listened quietly without replying to a businessman turned non-profit leader who was obviously finding frustration in his new role.

When he left the Foundation for Women several months later, the situation was not good for our work. And so I turned to my father who has been an entrepreneur and successful businessman his entire life. I seemed to recall that there was a period in his sixties where a business reality surprised him. Now that he is in his eighties and on the other side of it, I wanted and needed his wisdom.

Yes it had been quite a surprise and quite a period for him then. My father had to ask my mother to help him. He had to ask colleagues to help him. He had to ask God to help him. I am doing all of that right now. And as happened in my father's case, help is appearing and the light is returning.

And one of the dearest bonuses of this period is closing the circle with my parents. I have never fit in my biological family – felt a much different calling than my parents and four sisters – have traveled the world and been an advocate for social change for things none of them have ever seen. My parents now get that I have made a significant impact on the world for the better; that I have been able to do something very positive. They like sharing what I do with members of their Bible Study Group with joy and admiration.

So this situation gave them a gift – a chance for them to help the Foundation for Women through this *"bad things happen to good people"* period. They have become a life raft as we make a recovery plan to move forward which will only be enhanced by the present circumstances. Joy for them; great gratitude for me.

Betrayal

Upon returning home from a spiritual adventure to Peru in recognition of the end of the Mayan calendar in December 2012, I received a call from a dear friend. *"I am quitting the Foundation for Women."* What? *"I am quitting the Foundation for Women."* Of course I want to respect the feelings of others and not argue with them, but this totally took my breath away.

I finally said *"Could you please come in Friday and speak with me in person?"* She agreed – but also wrote an impersonal letter to our entire team in San Diego and Liberia explaining how she didn't feel she had or was making a difference. Great surprise and sadness rocked everyone.

That was a long time ago and we have not had a conversation since – after five years of deep conversations and connections, after trusting her with my life, after our work together at the Foundation for Women, and after naming her as executor of my personal trust.

I muse on what happened. Did she make a choice when I was out of the country to turn her back and her life on her Foundation for Women family of many years; to commit to a man with money who had not been able to achieve at the Foundation for Women what he expected so was off to start his own non-profit organization?

The great surprise and sadness is gone. Our time together was obviously complete this life time. I am holding her in my heart of compassion. I have found gratitude for the experience. I now intimately know what betrayal and grief feel like. I have great compassion for others who must experience surprising and devastating loss. And I am committed to never acting in such a way to another human being, this life time or any others; instead always turning into the conversation however difficult that may be instead of walking away.

Gratitude always – this time learning from heartbreak.

Opportunity for Service

We connected after many false starts. When we finally had a conversation which I thought would be ten minutes, it lasted more than an hour and we both cried several times.

We were sisters who had not until then met. She had grown up in San Diego and moved away as a child. I had come to San Diego after childhood to my adult home. A match so blessed it seemed.

We dreamed together. I opened my home, my life, my rolodex in the US and in Liberia. The plans were mighty and grand.

My commitment to the poorest of the poor continued in Liberia and around the globe. I did not wait for a silver bullet as Dr. Yunus would say. I kept on doing service to those whose voices are not heard while our dreaming happened. I did not stop being of service while the big plans were being formulated in our conversations.

Things did not progress in the grand scheme as anticipated. So I opened more fully, asking a dear friend to contribute to *"Seats at the Table for Liberia"* to get our collaboration launched. That initial money led to more money led to more help led to…

Silence.

Now, there is no speaking after so much intimacy and connection and commitment. She has taken another path, surely a better money decision; our conversations stopped after the other money arrived.

Epiphany today in the shower – always grateful. This was another opportunity to be of service and I am so grateful for that. I had been stuck in *"If it wasn't for me, they would have been bankrupt"* thinking instead of being of service. Now that thinking has been transformed into *"How wonderful that I had another opportunity to be of service – and I am praying for their highest good and the highest good of all beings."*

My resentment was never realized by her; it only affected me. The release is lightening and transformative and freeing. I pray for the peace and happiness of all beings every day – and know that everyone is truly doing the best they can at any one moment, or they would do better. There is comfort in that knowing.

Gratitude always.

Murray Died

In September I went to Murray as I needed his wisdom. I have known Murray more than a decade and secretly in my heart refer to him as *"my wisdom man."* We haven't had long conversations regularly over the years. But any time I have called and asked to see him, he has made himself available.

This September I "knew" that his wisdom needed to join the conversation regarding the Foundation for Women's domestic poverty eradication work. He opened his home and his heart and his wisdom to me and two colleagues for nearly two hours. He came up with an idea. He would host a luncheon before his family's Thanksgiving holiday for several key people and philanthropists in town who might not be aware of our work, or if they were, could use an up-date.

The luncheon happened in a private dining room mid-November. It was truly special. Murray and I made a commitment to make a follow-up plan once he and his family were back from a holiday in Hawaii.

Early December, true to his word as always, Murray opened his office and afternoon to me and a colleague. A plan was in the making and he would begin the connections with all who attended or were invited but could not come. He sent me off to Peru with a bear hug and reassurance that all is and would be wonderful!

Just before I left the country a few days later, I heard that Murray might have to go into the hospital for a small health issue. I sent him a card of concern. When I returned to La Jolla, I found out that yes, he did have to be hospitalized, that all was well and that he was to be discharged the following day. I sent him another card expressing my joy that whatever is was, it was over and that he was on his way home. Tomorrow came – and in the process of coming home, Murray died. Just like that, totally unexpected. Gone.

I, like thousands, lost my breath in total disbelief and grief. I have done a lot of hospice work this life time – I know death is part of life. It happens. But somehow this was so wrong…

Murray had a way of making every conversation he had appear to be the most important one he had ever had, a way of making the person he was speaking with feel as if they were the most important person he knew. I felt that way with Murray. The hundreds and hundreds of people who attended his celebration of life all felt that way I am sure. In our collective grief, one of his friends spoke and recommended that together we all remember in any given moment WWMD – What Would Murray Do.

WWMD is with me constantly. I want to be present with and honor people as Murray did. I want to leave a legacy of goodness as Murray did. I want to leave the planet in a better state as Murray did.

I am beyond grateful and blessed to have known Murray.

The Knock

Two weeks before a long anticipated and much needed time-out in Kauai was to happen, the unexpected happened. The knock at the door. He was there, my spirit partner, unexpectedly.

He came in, sat down and announced that he not only was not going to Kauai but also was not available for our partner-lover-best friend relationship any longer. He cried as he explained that he was tired of disappointing people, himself included. He had to find his way through a crisis that he had created in every aspect of his life. He was leaving.

I listened and offered the Kleenex box – and finally said "I know." He left.

For many years we had experienced the spectrum of travel around the world, deep conversations, great imaginings regarding my work and his many projects, shared brilliance, love, and chaos. Once during those years I left the relationship when the chaos became too much. But a sincere apology and a committed meditation and yoga practice by him drew me back in.

I knew this was not a request for a temporary time out. I felt as though I had been hit by a truck. It was different than the endings of other relationships in my life because at a very deep level I knew we were spirit partners, that we signed up for big lessons this life time, and that we are learning them with help from each other.

Yet amazingly my initial recovery time was surprisingly short. I was "directed" to dear friend Loie who is one of the wisest women in my life, to reconnecting with and reviewing a healing session I had experienced a couple of years previously – and to *The Mastery of Love"* by Don Miguel Ruiz. The bigger picture instead of the chaos of the moment appeared. Breathing. Trusting. Loving.

Little did I know then that he was leaving for another woman, that we would reconnect, that he would leave two years later for her again, that there was more learning…

I believe all is and continues to happen for the highest good of all beings. I am choosing gratitude.

Where are the women??

I started this adventure – the Foundation for Women – nearly 20 years ago now. I so wanted a family and community. And the response was amazing! Our first gathering in April 1998 drew hundreds of women – and they came and came and came for years. We had started a movement. And then they stopped coming.

Those in need of our microfinance support grew in number in India where we first funded and then in Zambia, South Africa and Niger. Then they appeared in a big way in Liberia, West Africa. Those in need also appeared in San Diego – hundreds and thousands of women locally and globally to whom we as a community, a movement, gave hope and a life-line. And then the women of our Foundation for Women community stopped coming.

Challenging economic times began in 2008. Daily deposits at the Foundation for Women stopped. Philanthropy changed. A capacity building grant in 2010 brought staff to replace volunteers at the Foundation for Women along with an ambitious and unrealistic growth plan. Our donor community began to shrink further.

Then an accomplished business man joined our non-profit cause and changed a circle of conversation into a triangle with him at the top. After several months of frustration, he left – with key Foundation for Women leaders – and he left behind a mountain of debt.

Where are the women who built the Foundation for Women community and movement? Where are the women who stayed in conversation regularly? Where are the women who collectively did so much more than any one of us could have done individually? Where are the women who were my family, my core, my forever-count-on women who I knew had my back? Where are the women when I need them now?

Perhaps I believed in the wrong women – those that followed the man with the money – instead of women willing to hold hands with each other to create a new way of being when things become challenging, those who dream of a new paradigm where all women's voices are heard, those who know there is a new way possible with women joining hands together.

Where are the women? I am sad they are gone and I am accepting reality. Those who remain continue to believe. And I await the arrival of more who share the dream of a new way of being for all women, those who will never give up.

I will never give up. I have a special quote from the Dalai Lama next to one of my favorite Buddha statues:

Never Give Up

No matter what is going on

Never give up

Develop the heart

Too much energy in your country

is spent developing the mind

instead of the heart

Develop the heart

Be compassionate

Not just to your friends

but to everyone

Be compassionate

Work for peace

in your heart and in the world

Work for peace

and I say again

Never give up

No matter what is happening

No matter what is going on around you

Never give up

– H.H. The XIV Dalai Lama

Gratitude always.

Chapter 5

Women's Circles

It is all so much bigger than me...

This life time and all the work is so much bigger than me and my personal story. I am doing all I do for all women and girls, including me. I am working on my personal healing on behalf of all women and girls. I am the stone in the pond with ripples going out into the cosmos.

This gives me such strength to continue when at times I want to crawl in bed and bring the covers over my head. "Just take the next step Deborah." "Just do the next indicated thing Deborah." So much more than me.

I know that I volunteered this lifetime to help be the voice for women whose voices are not heard; this is my story from the beginning of this incarnation. It has not been easy this commitment. At times I have questioned and wavered. Yet I have never stepped back from or abandoned the commitment. It is all so much bigger than me.

Holding hands with my spiritual sisters all over the globe has given me such inspiration and the energy to get up every day and do what needs to be done for all of those in much greater need than me, particularly women and girls. My sobbing with sadness moments come and go – as I have wonderful shelter and enough food and clothing and all the essentials at the bottom of the Maslow's hierarchy of needs pyramid. I have been blessed all of my life to be able to deal with those things beyond physical survival.

And my lessons this lifetime have been so big – but I have been able to process them in the special community of La Jolla, California by the sea and with the amazing support of my spiritual teacher and anchor Verniece. I am beyond blessed and will not waver from my commitment until all women and girls the world over can say, "I am beyond blessed."

So beyond grateful to be of service this lifetime... Thank you Divine Mother.

"Ending Violence Against Women and Girls"

I am a delegate again here at the UN and overwhelmed and blessed and full of great grief and great hope – all due to the stories and connections with my global sisters.

One in three women on the planet will experience sexual violence in her life time – I am the one in three. My story, which begins with the violation of my body in the 5th grade by my teacher, pales to the horrific stories of rape and torture from *"The International Campaign to Stop Rape & Gender Violence in Conflict,"* an effort which I joined today as an individual and as the Foundation for Women and FFW Liberia.

I sat in a circle of women this morning all committed to *"Women as Spiritual Leaders: Transforming Violence"* and gasped inside as I realized that ending violence against women begins with me ending violence against myself – ending all thoughts and behaviors that are abusive and not in support of my highest good.

I welcomed Samrica from Liberia to the UN this afternoon and to America for the first time ever! She has stubs for feet and her right hand; her left hand is the only fully developed and functioning body limb. Yet she is so full of joy and possibility and wonder!

The statistics and stories are profound and overwhelming. So I came home this evening to my safe and secure hotel sanctuary filled with *"Am I doing enough? Is the Foundation for Women doing enough? Why is this all happening and I am not doing more??"*

And I heard in my silence and quiet – *"Just do more of what you are doing – microfinance locally and globally. You cannot right all the wrongs of the world; do more of what you do best. And hold hands in circles with your sisters in solidarity who are doing other social change and justice work.*

Women together = miracles!

I am so grateful for this female incarnation, for my global sisters, for my opportunity to be of service…

The Midwives

Friend Jan and I became midwives in service to the world again today. We became a tight circle of amazing women with Samrica from Liberia.

We all are social change agents, social justice champions and women leaders. I am committed to supporting all the women on the planet whose voices are not heard; to helping to eliminate global poverty through microfinance. Jan is a prolific writer, teacher, song writer and performer, and photographer. Samrica is a member of the Foundation for Women Liberia, new wife and mother, and major champion for the physically handicapped as that is her reality this lifetime.

Today Samrica was a princess dressed in a new deep blue sleeveless mini-skirted dress. She bit the price tag off with her teeth before dropping her jeans and t-shirt on the bathroom floor to transform herself into a model for Jan's photographic eye and camera. Her African hair was newly done with extensions and fell softly over her right shoulder. She applied special makeup to enhance the photo session which was about to document her brief life in America.

Samrica is staying at the home of one of our donors to the Foundation for Women in my community of La Jolla as Michelle's guest. Samrica first came here last year after I introduced them to each other at the UN Commission on the Status of Women. Michelle offered to connect her to handicapped sports specialists to see if something other than socks could be worn on her stubs for feet and brought her to La Jolla. Samrica is back again this year to evaluate what she has been wearing on her stubs and to see if something "more fashionable" than the heavy black boots, albeit with a Gucci emblem on the toes, could be created.

Today we documented Samrica's reality in America versus her reality in Liberia. She is in a mansion on six-acres overlooking Black's Beach. In Liberia she lives is a space smaller than one garage with a tin roof that leaks. Instead of her mattress on the floor there which she shares with her husband and daughter, she is for two more nights in an amazing suite with a huge bed and adjoining bath overlooking the Pacific Ocean. She has come to know both ends of the bell-shaped curve regarding living circumstances.

Jan took more than 200 photos today beginning in Samrica's bedroom, then in the house and gardens, by the pool and amazing artwork, and from outposts over-looking the sea. Samrica will be able to share her California reality with those in Liberia in a photo book soon. How does she integrate this extreme? How will her family and friends in Liberia? Jan and I wonder.

And as our afternoon circle ended, it gave Jan and me an opportunity to have a deep heart conversation about our individual realities, how our worlds are all so different and yet so connected. Love. Integrity. Practice. Belief. Trust. Connection. Gratitude.

I am divorced for more than 20 years and aching for a true spirit partner human connection. Jan recently lost her life partner Annie to throat cancer and also has no soft place to land. Samrica is living in a country devastated by senseless civil war for almost two decades and lives on less than $1/day when in Liberia – and is married to the man of her dreams and has a daughter she adores.

Jan, Samrica and I are a circle of women, an amazing circle of women. We were in circle in Liberia a few months ago and then again today in America. A miracle. A mystery. Gratitude always.

One Billion Rising

There is an amazing global shift happening. A new way of being is emerging with women leading the way.

On Valentine's Day February 14, 2013 women all around the globe stood up in support of changing an awful reality. One in three women on the planet will experience rape or brutality during her lifetime. I have experienced date rape and brutality from a man.

Seventy-five percent of the women in the country of Liberia have been raped as tragically rape continues to be used as a weapon of war throughout the African continent and beyond.

All of this is not OK with me. Like the statistics of poverty, something I thought I could do nothing about…

Now that is not the case. I am part of a movement of women to create a totally different reality with dancing and joy and celebration of sisterhood.

I am so grateful to be on the planet right now – to be part of major social change for women and girls, to be part of the global moment in support of women and girls and the global commitment to end poverty.

Of all the things I could be doing and all the places I could be doing it, I am keenly aware of how Divine Mother is guiding my steps, and my heart is bursting with gratitude to be of service to so many in the US and around the globe.

Pinch me – such a blessing. So grateful.

Sunday Morning Sacred

Sunday mornings have always been sacred for me, ever since I left the Sunday school and mandatory church attendance behind as a teenager. I treasure the quiet meditation and prayer time, the reflective silence, the listening to Divine Mother. And over the many years I have come to treasure the solitude instead of ache with loneliness.

This Sunday morning I awoke with a hole in my heart and so wished there was someone next to me to just hold me. Loneliness instead of solitude was front and center. So after my prayer and meditation time, I put on my shoes and set off for a long walk by the sea. Loneliness came with me as I watched families interacting, couples holding hands. So I did what I have come to do in such a moment – notice it, surround it with loving-kindness and compassion, and turn my attention to my gratitude list.

A young girl with a bright t-shirt exclaiming, *"Dream it! Believe it! Achieve it!"* passed me. Yes, anything is possible! And I began reviewing my gratitude list:

I am grateful to be living in La Jolla by the sea. How did I ever get here from the cornfields of the Midwest and now for several decades!

I am grateful for the fabulous work I am so blessed to do through the Foundation for Women here in San Diego and all around the globe, particularly in Liberia. I am so very glad that I listened to Divine Mother nearly 20 years ago and made a commitment to service in a very different way than I had been doing.

I am grateful for my health and lifestyle, one of daily exercise and a vegetarian diet, for my entire adult life.

I am grateful for my dear and special friends like Loie who is now 80; we spent hours together on Valentine's Day sharing memories and love and sorrows and joy.

I am grateful for all the big lessons I signed up for that have taught me so very much – having an abusive mother has taught me compassion and forgiveness; a series of unavailable relationships has taught me to honor and value me before I can expect others to do that; screaming with pain and having no one hear my voice has brought me to be of service to other women whose voices are not being heard all over the globe.

I am grateful for my spiritual practice and my commitment to being a bodhi-sattva, a vow I renew each morning. *"I dedicate this day and all my thoughts and words and actions to the highest good of all beings. Realizing that sentient beings are numberless, I pray for the enlightenment of them all. I do release any personal merit I may have gained this lifetime toward that end, with total and complete sincerity and joy."*

I am grateful to be part of a tribe of women, circles of women so committed to making big goodness happen in the world.

Beyond blessed and grateful…

Dance Class

The knowing of never fitting in, such a huge knowing… Never feeling truly connected or feeling part of…

In the 1990's I took a dance class for the first time in my life. I always wanted to dance but never had the opportunity. I remember thinking immediately, *"If I could move my body in ways it has never moved before, maybe I could move my life in ways it has never moved before."* I loved NIA and it did take my life in ways I had never been able to imagine.

Since that first class, almost twenty years have passed. And my life has moved in ways it had never moved before. I have spent a lot of time in prayer and meditation – listening.

I birthed the Foundation for Women. I have traveled the world on a mission to eliminate global poverty through microcredit. I have worked in India, Zambia, South Africa, Niger and now in Liberia – places I had never dreamed of being when I first took that dance class.

I have created and been part of many women's circles all over the world. I have made many dear friends, lost some I thought would be part of my life forever, been betrayed by a few.

As a new year begins, my journal pages are blank, waiting to be filled with the mystery of what is yet to be. There is one certainty – there will forever be women's circles in my life. I know that Divine Mother "did not bring me this far to have me land on my head" as my spiritual teacher Verniece reminded as the challenging year of 2013 was ending. It is circles of women that sustain me – in my global microfinance work, my Course in Miracles commitment, my core circle of women friends, my global community of sisters around the world.

I am so grateful.

A Course in Miracles

In November 2012, I met a new friend for lunch on Coronado Island. Dolores had found her way to the Foundation for Women after her Soroptimist Club honored us and our work with an award.

We spoke of many things over that lunch as we got better acquainted. I loved Dolores instantly; her fun style with dyed blue streaks running through her beautiful gray hair and her bold jewelry, her infectious smile, and her truly loving spirit.

After we had covered many topics, she mentioned that she was thinking of starting a course in miracles group in January 2013. I instantly said, *"Count me in!"* I had known of the Course for many years but had never read or studied it. And how wonderful the thought to be part of a women's circle that I did not organize!

I had no idea then, but this was being presented at the beginning of 18 months of the biggest transformation of my life; here was a new spiritual safety container to hold me as I would walk through one unbelievable situation after another in the months ahead... A miracle.

Our circle has been meeting for months now, every Monday evening. This Monday circle is sacred; there is no conversation about ending it. There are eleven of us, all women. We have a bond that is held together by our individual commitments to choose love instead of fear, Spirit instead of ego. We are now forever holding hands as we walk this spiritual adventure together. So beyond dear.

All have been a witness to these last amazingly transformative months; all beacons of light and support. Sue always reminds me, *"If it's not okay, it is not over."* Such comfort.

Thank you dearest sisters for your love and compassion and commitment and presence in my life. My heart is so full of gratitude for each of you.

Intoxicated with Joy

I have arrived in the Land of Joy! I am beyond amazed and delighted and grateful!

The 2013 Alchemy women's gathering in San Francisco is a tipping point. I am present in a "basket container" of committed spiritual women from Thursday evening until Sunday noon – a beyond sweet and special container that brings clarity, brings peace.

In one circle gathering together, I heard my dear friend Kathe share that she knew at an early age she needed to lower her vibrational energy in order to be connected with others; that she had done that much of her life in order to fit – until now. Now she knows her true reality and is gathering the women.

Kathe's story is my story. We are both gathering the women – here in America, and I am also in Africa. It is so sweet the container that appears when women come together in circle. Miracles happen – as well as unbelievable insights and surprises. And all is held in the sacred container of women coming together in circle.

Freedom is appearing for the first time in my life. I have experienced others creating endings in my life – and ever so painful they have been. No more. I am committed to creating my own reality – letting go of what does not support me and the highest good of all beings. Like the microfinance women I have been supporting around the globe for almost two decades, I am in control of my destiny and my power and my reality – and my attitude of gratitude.

Women together = miracles! I have always known this and always shared this knowing. Now I believe this in my soul. The Alchemy gathering illuminated this reality for me in the most powerful way. Being held for several days in a container of love and hope and joy and peace filled with fabulous women from every age and race and reality totally filled me with the joy of infinite possibility.

Together we bowed to you Divine Mother and you Mother Earth in such reverence and appreciation in every conversation.

And this filled with me hope and faith before the next unimaginable happened in my life just months later… Beyond grateful.

In a Circle of Fabulous Women

We have assembled a fabulous circle of women in this special cottage where I surprisingly find myself Divine Mother; a circle of women from all over the world reflecting our global sisterhood.

"Tucson" was created by dear artist friend Kioko in Kenya from scrap metal that would have littered the earth but instead became an expression of great feminine power and beauty. She has dreadlocks made from metal chains and a necklace of sparkplugs – and is so beautiful.

Also from Kenya, "Masai Sisters" stand tall and proud with their walking sticks.

"Spirit" is a patchwork of red fabric scraps with a single round button for her face, made by a grantee of the New Mexico Women's Foundation.

"Cornmaiden" from Santa Fe fits in my palm and is a beautiful translucent blue stone with one red spot at her heart center.

"Hope" is from Cameroon, made by the Namji people. She is a wooden, red-beaded beauty with cowrie shells making her afro hairstyle.

"Quan Yin" is encased in glass and a divine expression of the feminine spirit of love and compassion; a gift from dear Feng Shui colleague Cathleen.

"Zoey" is about four feet tall, a beaded beauty from Africa wearing green sneakers and a bright red round hat. She is the wise elder of this circle.

"Emily" is a patchwork of discarded fabric scraps made into a beautiful doll with bright red hair, an infectious smile and pink cheeks.

"Joyce" is a work of art from South Africa standing tall in her mini-skirt and halter top. Pure joy.

"The Moms" are both beaded beauties holding their small daughters close to their chests.

"Africa, Bride and Peace" were all created by the Ndebele people in South Africa. Africa came to the US many years ago, wrapped in bubble wrap and tenderly carried across the globe on an airplane. Bride joined our circle after we met at the African Museum at the Smithsonian Museum. Peace was a gift from a dear friend in Santa Fe. They all have multiple metal rings stretching their necks and are adorned with bright multi-color beads.

Two more Masai women stand proudly on a table next to the Buddha fountain. "Present and Moment" complete this fabulous circle of women.

I am so blessed to be part of this fabulous circle of women, so blessed to be part of the global sisterhood of women.

Tremendous gratitude.

Chapter 6

Self Reflection

Sometimes it takes my breath away...

I had a quiet "Deborah Day" yesterday – just me and the sea and meditation and reading and resting, a day of being versus doing. So fabulous. Why don't I schedule more of them??

Awakening this morning early to a stormy sky and sea, I see a patch of blue sky way out amid the clouds over the ocean. It is such a physical reminder that despite the chaos and darkness, the light is always there.

This quiet early morning I am reflecting on all the darkness I have lived through and marvel at the fact that I am still on this planet. Regular childhood episodes of soap being rubbed in my mouth because I did not speak correctly, constant reminders that I was a horrible example for my younger sisters, grounded for months at a time, accusations of awful behavior I would never dream of doing – the prison of an abusive childhood. Yet I did survive.

Now that I am always able to find gratitude, I look back at my mother and hold her with great compassion. A terrified young woman found herself with five daughters by the time she was 26 years old – a baby trying to raise babies. I have nothing but loving-kindness and compassion for her now.

As the oldest daughter, I became the parent to my younger sisters, an emotional partner for my father – and I experienced a deep knowing that I was in a "foreign place" devoid of kindness and quiet and peace and love that I ached for.

Now acceptance. I know I volunteered for the lessons of spending time in the darkness, of learning forgiveness and compassion, of being grateful for all.

Still sometimes it all takes my breath away…

Addicted to Doing

I am addicted to doing. Every day I try to prove to God and the Angels that it is okay for me to be on the planet. I have to justify my existence.

I learned as a young child that I was never good enough, never okay. I never behaved correctly; stayed in my room too much; didn't say the right things; questioned too much; never fit. So I have been striving and achieving my entire life to be okay, to be enough.

Exhausting.

In the chaos of a several-year relationship, I found my way to Dr. Paul Brenner. In just a few minutes he drew my life story on a piece of blank white paper. Clear. My mother this, my father this, my siblings this. *"Everyone has addictions,"* he said, *"Yours is to doing, to prove it is okay to be here."*

I see this. I understand it. It all makes sense to me. That important conversation was years ago and I am still addicted to doing, although I am ever so much more mindful about my addiction.

My lists are long. My calendar is full. I am still trying to prove that I am okay to be here. It is exhausting. But I am learning to "be" with my doing, to notice when it is happening, to surround it with loving-kindness and compassion, to be patient with it instead of driven by it.

I am grateful for the awareness of my doing addiction and my mindfulness practice – and for developing self-kindness instead of self-criticism. I am making progress toward a balance of being and doing – a wonderful journey. So grateful…

A Lesson in Mindfulness

I am a busy person – and I count on things to work when I need them to.

A beyond beautiful summer day appeared in San Diego after days of fog and gloom. So I opened the sun-visor on my car roof with great joy of letting warm, sunny air in – so happy!

When I went to leave my office, the temperatures had risen, I felt drawn to the air conditioning instead of fresh air. I tried to close the roof top vent and found it not working.

What?

Everything is America works. I spend so much time in Africa and elsewhere where things do not work. When I am in America things work.

Try as I might for several minutes I could not make the sun visor behave as I wanted and needed – so I let go and…

AND I planned how I would fix the broken sun-visor. I would take the car to Shawn, the mechanic I know and trust at the gas station. I will pay him whatever he says. I will accept whatever Shawn says and not worry about the cost.

And then I arrived at Mary's, my nutritionist, and tried one more time to close the sun-visor – and it closed easily.

All of my expectations of disaster and needed car repair vanished. I was back to the present moment. I was reminded of Einstein's quote that *"98% of the disasters in my life never happened – they were all in my mind."*

I am grateful for the mindfulness reminder, yet again.

Being Present

Being present does not come easy for me. I have to continually work at being mindful, being present.

I have found several ways this life time to escape. It has not been easy being in this skin this incarnation.

When I first found meditation nearly 40 years ago it became a way to go away.

The unavailable people in my life taught me how to use wine to go away. I learned well.

My love of running, marathon after marathon, kept me moving away from being right here, right now.

Airplanes have taken me away for most of my adult life.

A multitude of books, constant reading, has taken be away.

I need reminders to be present. My sacred space holds many mindfulness bowls; inviting the bowl to sound brings me back to my next breath. I learned years ago from one of my dearest teacher, Thich Nhat Hanh, to use the ringing of the telephone as a mindfulness reminder. My many Buddhas remind me to come back to my next breath. The poetry of Hafiz helps me be present. My treasured photo of His Holiness the Dalai Lama is a reminder. It is not easy for me to be present. I need lots of help. I am so grateful I have many reminders.

Just sit...

I didn't want to go out for my walk by the sea this morning. It is a cold overcast February morning with big rain coming. But I forced myself to go, wanting to say my prayers outside as I always do each morning.

As I started to speak the prayer, a rush of tears came. From where? The stress of the last several months has been the biggest of my life. A dear friend is away for several weeks so a key support system is absent. An early morning email confirmed the challenges of the moment. All certainly a part of the present overwhelm.

Then a special thought. The failed hostile takeover attempt of the Foundation for Women is really the ultimate form of flattery. The "J Team" wanted what we have had for the last 15+ years – a community, a way to give service to those in need, respect and appreciation by so many, a sense of truly making a difference. What a special thought Divine Mother. I offered more prayers for the "J Team."

And then I noticed scattered along the bluff something I had never seen in more than 35 years of running or walking by the sea in the morning. People just sitting – meditating – quietly being by the sea. There were more than a dozen. Young people, perhaps late teens, just sitting. I got the message so clearly Divine Mother – just go sit. It is what I wanted to do but I felt I needed to do something else. Want versus need.

I am back in my spiritual sanctuary overlooking the sea instead of out next to it and ready to just sit.

I am so grateful.

Nothing but Angels

There is a special children's book *"The Little Soul and the Sun"* which I love to pick up regularly. It is a reminder that we all are beams of light and goodness – everyone, everywhere.

This is a wonderful thought and not easily remembered. I come back to this practice again and again – seeing the light and goodness in everyone. Every-one is doing the best they can, including me.

The message of the book helps me find gratitude in every circumstance and situation with myself and all beings. I believe that God has sent nothing but angels to me, that all beings are behaving just as they need to so I can always come from a place of love and compassion and kindness and forgiveness – and gratitude.

Only I Can Give Myself Permission

After months of non-stop travel, I am home in my spiritual sanctuary by the sea for nearly three weeks before having to connect with yet another airplane, a mode of transportation that seems to have become my constant companion.

I awoke this morning quietly. After reading poet David Whyte lately, I am struck by how important the early morning time is for me. Like David, I treasure the morning for spiritual practice and writing and peace before moving on to the next parts of my day.

This morning, however, the "knowing" was bigger than a thought – it was a necessity. *"I must have hours of quiet prayer and meditation and reading and writing before I can do anything else today."* I could not make my body move toward my shoes to begin the day with exercise as I have for decades. I could not make my hands open my computer or look at my blackberry. I "knew" I had to be quiet.

I lit a candle, curled up with a cup of tea in my favorite chair draped in my cherished meditation shawl and sat…and sat some more…and sat some more. Clarity. Only I can give myself permission for this spiritual time at dawn. Only I can honor myself in this way. Only I can make the choice to be present with the quiet and stillness.

My addiction to doing is great. My To Do List long. There are so many reasons why not to take this time. I am not entertaining them anymore. Only I can give myself permission for this time – and I am so worth it. I deserve it. I now demand it. I am so grateful.

Journals

I have kept a journal for more than 35 years. I have files full of yellow legal pads filled with nearly daily writings.

Sue Bender says in her book *"Everyday Sacred"* that *"writing is the best way I've found so far to look at my life and tell the truth."*

That's what I have done. When it goes down on paper, it gets out of my head. It is the truth regardless of how much I want to pretend it is not. Thank you Myrna for suggesting I put it on paper so long ago now.

I am so grateful…

"If it was easy, someone would have done it already!"

My dear friend Jack has been reminding me of this since the day I started the work of the Foundation for Women. Now almost two decades into a movement to eliminate global poverty through microcredit, I am reminding myself.

We are at a critical time in this work of the Foundation for Women. After years of being a grant-making organization by raising money and funding microcredit programs in several places around the world, we turned to being an operator in 2007. No longer financially supporting microfinance organizations, we are now the microfinance organization that thousands of poor women rely on. What a difference!

And after years now, we find the organization and the work at a critical juncture. Yesterday I listened to a member of our FFW team say directly to me, *"It is all your fault Deborah – you have to take responsibility for the present state of the organization and the work. Your optimism is denial."* I listened and nodded my head while doing my best to not take the stress-filled comments personally.

Yikes what a journey this lifetime! I am so committed to my bodhisattva pledge which I speak aloud every morning – May all I do today be for the highest good of all beings – and try to stay present with that commitment throughout the day. I know intellectually that everything is divinely ideal at every moment. I know to not take anything personally, that other people's stories are their stories and have nothing to do with me.

So I concentrate on gratitude always. The recent interchange reminded me yet again that gratitude is the only way of being, no matter what the circumstances. And Jack's wisdom echoes in my knowingness – *"If it was easy, someone would have done it already."* And I find peace.

So grateful for Angel Jack.

Cultivating kindness for me

Another birthday is approaching and I am surprised again – how could I have been on this planet for so long, be of this age, and still not have a committed relationship/partnership? The lessons keep coming – the learning all good – but at the end of the day I crawl in bed by myself.

I practice loving-kindness and acceptance. And I trust that all is happening just as it needs to for me and the highest good of all beings.

It is a hard lesson, loving-kindness for me. My prayers have so often been focused on the trauma and suffering in India and now Africa. What do I have to even think about regarding myself when there is so much suffering so beyond my existence?

In truth, it starts with me. I must be peaceful with me before there will be peace in the world. I know that – so believe that – am so committed to that. I, as one human being, can help create peace and hope by having that myself.

I am so grateful always for my spiritual practice.

By the sea

It is a quiet Saturday morning – just me and the sea and quiet.

The wonder of it all. How did a young girl born into a family in a small town in the middle of the US end up in a sacred space overlooking the sea in Southern California?

What a spiritual adventure. I thank God, my band of angels and all Buddhas and all Enlightened Ones each day for this miracle. It is so very clear to me that

I have help, that my steps are truly being guided.

I know that I signed up for big work and big lessons this life time. I am grateful for the opportunity to clean some karma, to be of service, to contribute to the highest good of all beings.

And I get to do it here by the sea – so amazing.

A few years ago, I thought I needed to experience living in a house. I left the sea, rented the sacred space and moved up the hill where I could see the sea in the far distance. Once that experience was complete, I was guided back home to the sea. A miracle. I could not have made that happen.

As I look out to the sea while writing this, my amazement is palpable. I am here, right now, this moment in my sacred space by the sea. I am so grateful.

It's Not What I Wanted...

I have been so very blessed to have been touched by amazing teachers. In fact, every person who has been in my life has been my teacher. I now realize that.

Jack Kornfield said at the first meditation retreat I ever sat with him, *"This is your practice: Everyone on the planet is enlightened except you and everyone is doing exactly what they need to be doing so that you will become enlightened."* Quite a thought.

Just when I think that I have reached a plateau, a moment to take a breath and survey the scenery, BAM another learning opportunity shows up – without warning. Without my spiritual practice and deep knowing, I would not be vertical. The lessons often knock me completely over, but now only temporarily. I can go back to the teachings and learning that are so much a part of me.

I have a very favorite Sylvia Boorstein quote: *"It's not what I wanted but it is what I've got; I don't know if it is good or bad; I will have to wait to find out."*

Isn't that really it, over and over and over again?? In each moment, I don't know if what I am experiencing is good or bad, but I know I will find out. Life happens. Some things appear good, some things not so good. And I always find out.

I had an epiphany walking along the beach this morning. I am in a period of grief due to the loss of a relationship that was deeply impactful in my life. I was thinking of Sylvia's wisdom – and then aha! Maybe this is exactly what I wanted! Maybe I am not only healing and growing me, but I am healing all women who are not able to honor themselves and settle for "just OK" instead of "Fabulous!" Maybe this is exactly what I wanted!

What a joyful thought! So grateful!

Will it ever make sense?

The gift of age has given me a very different perspective than when I first went off to college, chose my first career, started my first business. My life is totally and completely all about service to others and the world; may all I do be for the highest good of all beings.

And at the same time I am wondering more and more – will it all ever make sense? What lessons did I sign up for this life time? Who are all these souls I am sharing this incarnation with? Why was I born where I was, live where I do, and travel the globe non-stop?

What a marvelous mystery this life is. I am so grateful for this moment, this life, this work I am beyond blessed to do, this spiritual sanctuary by the sea that I call home, this travel around the globe I do regularly – how grateful I am to be a global citizen.

It will be very interesting to see how all my life experiences make sense one day. But maybe they won't. For now I am grateful for everything as confusing as it all is… Gratitude always.

Chapter 7

Friends

Dr. Ari and dear Vishnu

I am in New York on my way back from Africa for the 25th Anniversary Celebration of the Global Fund for Women, a reception at the Clinton Global Initiative, some Women Moving Millions business and connections with dear and special friends – all big and wonderful – or so I thought until this afternoon.

In October of last year I attended a gathering in Italy – Awakened World 2012; Spirituality for the 21st Century. I was beyond blessed to meet wonderful people from all over the world, all committed to social change for the highest good of all beings. Among the 250 participants was a contingent from Sri Lanka led by Dr. Ariyaratne with among others his right hand companion of the last 13 years Vishnu.

Today in an Italian café by the Union Theological Seminary just west of Harlem and north of Columbia University, I received a lesson in pure wisdom from a gifted teacher. Dr. Ari explained that when one tries to effect social change, one goes through five stages as Gandhi detailed: *"First people will greet you with indifference; next they will ridicule you; then they will abuse you; next they will put you in jail, or even try to kill you. If you go through these four phases successfully, you will get to the most dangerous phase – when people start respecting you. Then you can become your own enemy unless you are careful."*

This enlightened 82-year-old spiritual master and teacher acknowledged my recent betrayals and said calmly, *"There will be many more dear Deborah."* Then Dr. Ari told me of grave transgressions by people he had trusted, one man in particular who he trusted completely for 24 years. So many episodes of unbelievable behavior by others… Despite all the goodness of his work and those he serves at the grassroots level in thousands of communities in his country, there are those who want to stop him. Though there have been attempts, he has not been jailed or killed – goodness does prevail in the end.

As he hugged me and touched my head when we separated, I felt a grace and peace flow through me that I have not experienced. I am not alone in believing and fostering tremendous social change as my spiritual practice. Dr. Ari and his dear aide Vishnu both see me as a fellow beam of light committed to service in support of a better world.

I am grateful for adversity transformed into learning resulting in such special blessings – that happened today! And for the membership I am embracing in a tribe of social change agents. With Dr. Ari and Vishnu's blessings, I now label myself a "compassionate activist." I am grateful to know that I am not alone in adversity and that I am now part of a very special community of compassionate activists welcomed today by two beyond dear men from Sri Lanka who just happened to be in New York at the same time I was.

By chance? There is no "chance" in this connection today. Hugs of gratitude to you Dr. Ari and to you Vishnu with great love and admiration.

Dear Friend Jack

We met in the middle 90's when we both were showing up in service to the La Jolla Town Council's Parks and Beaches Committee. We were both committed to preserving and protecting our precious La Jolla coastline. I never could have dreamed the impact that meeting would have on my life.

Jack has become one of the dearest people in my life. Aside from being a community volunteer, Jack was present for the first stages the Foundation for Women. He has been a trusted friend and wonderful supporter of me personally and the work for nearly two decades now.

And Jack is my hero. He never waivers from his consistent and ever-present positive attitude. It matters not what the circumstances or conversation – health or finances or relationships or weather or work or living spaces or travel or – Jack is always able to see the good in every situation. *"Attitude is everything; pick a good one,"* could have been created with Jack as the poster person.

I consider myself a positive person but nothing like Jack. I joke that I want a transfusion of his positive DNA regularly. He is such a model for always seeing the good, always choosing the positive, always feeling gratitude.

I am so beyond blessed by Jack's presence in my life; thank you Jack for so much! I am so filled with gratitude.

Opening my Heart

Eddie is an angel. Several years ago at a charity event, I "won" a gym membership and time with a trainer. I have always made exercise a very important aspect of my life, always belonged to a gym and made daily workouts part of my routine. So I accepted this gift with little anticipation; just another connection in support of my physical well-being.

Then I met Eddie. He began a routine to open my heart. Working out at a gym was about physical training. It previously had nothing to do with my heart. And now here I was focusing on my heart. Weight training with shoulders back, chest open. Yikes. I had not realized that physically I had been trying to keep my heart protected; emotionally, yes, but not physically.

My workouts became painful, but not physically. Shortly after I started working with Eddie, I showed up for a session in tears. Instead of staying at the gym,

Eddie guided me to the coffee house next door and sat with me, totally present. *"It's all okay Deborah"* he said with such knowing when I was feeling anything but okay.

We talked about a recent loss in my life, and how it had brought forward other losses, so many losses. We talked about how my natural reaction to loss in my life is to close, to suck it up, to put a brave face to the world and push forward. And how much my heart hurt under that instinctual reaction and façade; how I did not care for and hold my heart in compassion; how I did not honor the loss as I would so easily and readily do for someone else in such a place.

I have had years of training sessions with Eddie now, supposedly for my physical health and well-being. Truly my regular sessions with Eddie are about so much more than that. It is not easy for me to keep my heart open after decades of pushing through pain instead of being present with it, honoring it. Eddie is an angel who continually reminds me of a healthier way of being. I leave the gym with my heart open and present to what is.

I know that I was guided to Eddie. I am grateful.

The Dark Night of the Soul

I went to Brett for my hair appointment this week and there by his appointment book and telephone was a beautiful leather book by Saint John of the Cross, *"The Dark Night of the Soul."* I am in the dark night of my soul. Here in Brett's salon was confirmation and a life preserver being tossed my way.

Dear Brett is one of the most special spiritual beings on the planet. He does so much more than hair with every client. He prays for them when he is shampooing their hair. And he is totally committed to his spiritual path, health and well-being.

I love Brett. For more than a decade we have shared special spiritual conversations, intimate life experiences, treasured books and our Virgo horoscopes with each other.

He lent me the book when he was finished with my head saying, *"You need this more than I do right now – please take it."*

Brett is a dear and special angel in my life for whom I am beyond grateful. And I am so grateful to be present enough to realize our connection is so much more than about my hair...

Call from Mary

I was blessed to meet Mary at a special dinner party given in my honor in Toronto by my dear friend Margot. I so treasure both of these fabulous women!

Mary, who lives in Canmore, Canada, and I stay in contact via email and in person at our occasional Women Moving Millions events. Mary recently had the knowing to speak with me – so when she had time between skiing and skating and I was free after walking the beach in warm and sunny San Diego, we made a date to speak one Sunday afternoon.

Mary began by saying that she knew it was time for her to make a change, that one of her Foundation donors had agreed to provide money to hire someone to begin raising money for the Foundation, that she was crabby doing the same things she used to love, that she was listening…

"When did you start your Foundation Mary?" I inquired. *"Fifteen years ago,"* she replied. Amazing as that is how long it has been for me since I started the Foundation for Women.

The day before our conversation I had a very surprising knowing: I needed to change my role at the Foundation for Women which I birthed in the 1990's. The realization totally surprised me, but I stayed with the first knowing until it became a very deep and certain knowing. It was time for a change. Change my role – when? I am still listening for an answer; not forcing a solution.

The conversation with Mary was an immediate and powerful validation of the knowing that came to me yesterday; it is time for a change and here is a fellow visionary doing the same thing. I am not alone. And my knowing is real.

I surrender every day – may it all be your way, not my way. May it all be for the highest good of all beings. May I please be your bodhisattva again today? I know I am changing my role at the Foundation for Women after birthing and nurturing it for years. Whoever would have thought?? I trust completely and I am so grateful to know that my thoughts and words and actions are being guided, all in support of the highest good for all beings. So grateful!

My friend Gene

As I write this from Africa, my friend Gene is being celebrated in America. Gene died suddenly several days ago. I was not close to say goodbye. I am not close to join today in his celebration of life.

I loved Gene – for his heart, his talent, his commitment to his family, his energy for my work, for wanting to help in so many ways.

Just before I left on a long trip to Spain for the Global Microcredit Summit and to Liberia for several weeks, Gene and I spent many days together, particularly the Saturday before my departure. We dreamed together, looked at photos together, planned a course together – all to help the work of the Foundation for Women to eliminate global poverty through microcredit.

Gene was a genius and a humanitarian, and he was about to create the greatest set of projects to help all of those I know who are suffering in poverty in Africa and in America. He was excited and committed.

I left on that month-long trip with my new ipad that he insisted on and helped me purchase so I could as he said, *"Track all I am going to create now. The first e-book is already coming together!"*

I love you Gene. I am beyond grateful for your belief in me and the work of the Foundation for Women. Your contribution will always be part of our work – and your spirit with us forever. Tremendous gratitude.

Javier

Oh, how I love Javier! He is such a special soul!

I met Javier more than three decades ago now. He cleans windows. And he does so much more than that. He brings clarity and openness to life.

Javier was here at my spiritual sanctuary by the sea two days ago, in preparation for the Dark Night of the Soul time all day yesterday. He cleaned everything – the windows and mirrors and most importantly the views for the sunrise and the sunset. I was not prepared yesterday to appreciate all he did in service for me.

Today when the BIG WAVE has receded into the sea, I am in awe of his gift to me. There is clarity everywhere uncluttered by the dirt of the past. Such openness and beauty and joy everywhere from every vantage point!

The big wave was about the grief I was holding regarding the loss of everyone who has come and gone from the Foundation for Women and me over the last many years. There have been so many who so believed and then went on to their next "so believe." I have tried to not take it personally over the years, but in truth my human heart was carrying a burden. The departure of the beyond trusted "J Team" at the end of 2012 opened my heart to the many losses over the years. Their departure was the most dramatic and impactful, yet another bam below the knees.

Javier and his deep knowing and belief in me and my work set the stage for my deep clarity by making every window and mirror brilliantly clean. Clear. Open. An uncluttered space for new beautiful possibilities. A space for complete trust and confidence in a new and better future.

So much more than cleaning windows. I am beyond grateful for you Javier and our decades of friendship. You have no idea how much you have impacted my world and life and work – bringing such clarity regularly. I am committed to letting you know.

Gratitude always. And love.

Kevin as my teacher

When Kevin showed up in my life more than eight years ago now, my healer Verniece said, "You have been waiting for this your whole life." Really? I always thought he would have been taller and would go to the gym more.

After one tumultuous lesson after another, Kevin is no longer in my life. The learning is complete. I have learned to deal with and be comfortable with uncertainty.

This is a very big lesson. My mother was very controlling, always needing to have things just her way. I struggled with the strictness and rigidity. I longed for a caring, kind mother who didn't have so many rules. It took me many years and lots of work before I came to realize her behavior was ruled by fear. If it couldn't be safe and predictable, chaos might happen and then what?

I see that same piece in me now. Being comfortable with uncertainty is part of my mindfulness practice, being in the moment. I have come to a place of peace with all in the past – all the bricks in my foundation – and I have come to a place of peace with the future. I learned by being in relationship with Kevin that I just need to keep coming back to the next breath, just need to stay in this moment. And that all that is needed for my highest good will be provided, whether that is with Kevin or without.

I don't want to live in fear as my mother did. I want to be comfortable with uncertainty. Kevin is my teacher. I am grateful.

Kiana

We met in the Union Bank parking lot more than a decade ago as we were both on the way to a Foundation for Women event in La Jolla. We were sisters who had not met this lifetime until then; we both knew it.

Kiana is my "knowing" sister, forever reminding me that Spirit is in charge and guiding all possibilities. She is grounded in her steadfast belief, never wavering from trust in "show me" thinking.

Kiana grew up on Moloka'i and was raised by her grandmother. There is some story of no shoes for years. And she speaks of her grandmother always welcoming anyone into her home, always enough to share even though there never appeared to be enough for her and the children she cared for.

Always gratitude and always enough – that is my lesson from dearest Kiana.

Kiana and I have stayed connected; we are dear spirit sisters forever connected. We spoke tonight, she in Kauai now that she has moved home from the Mainland to her Hawaiian roots and me in California. We reflected on our lives now that we have the gift of years. I told her of the events of the last months – the betrayals, the losses, the move, the intruder – and we celebrated all in support of my needed learning.

I am at peace and so grateful, after the most dramatic and unbelievable time in my life. Thank you Spirit as Kiana says for showing me the way; thank you for my dearest sister Kiana. So grateful.

Love Accepted

The title of a special painting given by a special friend to Princeton this year in honor of her dear friend sparked a conversation this evening between Dasha and me. Our lives are so different in so many ways and so exactly the same in one core way – accepting love.

We are both very accomplished at giving. And yet at this age and stage in our lives, we still need and want to practice receiving.

What is that about? Why as the female half of the species do we give more than we receive? Is it in our DNA to be mothers? Neither Dasha nor I are biological mothers. Is it culturally passed on generation to generation? Dasha and I grew up in dramatically different biological circumstances and different countries. We now live very different lives still in different countries. And are so similar in this way.

What is so difficult about accepting love??

I suggested to Dasha tonight that we commit to sharing with each other one example each week of when we were able to accept love. She replied citing the fact that we had made overly ambitious commitments in the past, so how about once a month?

Walking home after our conversation I thought "What?" Noticing and accepting love only once a month? I thought, "No Dasha dear, not once a month, not once a week, but rather once a day, once a moment, every moment. I want to commit to accepting love every moment, feeling and accepting the love of the universe, being in love as a fish is in water always."

Seeing the divine and love in every moment, every experience, every person is my committed practice. And letting that love be accepted into my heart, letting it really land. I want to know what that feels like.

I am grateful for our conversation Dasha, and for our commitment to a practice of accepting love. I am holding your hand in our shared journey dear friend… very grateful.

Learning from Nature

I had lunch with my dear friend Jan yesterday. We do not connect in person regularly although we are always connected in spirit. We are both activists and social change agents and believers in a different kind of world.

My strong sense of urgency was part of our conversation. *"The time for change is now!"* Jan wisely reminded me to look to nature for guidance.

Across the street from my spiritual sanctuary, the roof of my neighbor Nick's house has become the birthing ground for three seagull chicks. I have been watching them for weeks now and wondering how it must be to come into this world on the roof of a house instead of some place soft and more welcoming. Each day the chicks grow a bit larger, practice spreading their wings a bit further, exert their individualism a bit more. They will fly in nature's divine timing. All is governed by divine timing.

I am grateful for Jan's wisdom and for the seagulls' reminder. I cannot make it different due to my sense of urgency. I can show up every day, do the best I can to make the world a better place, renew my commitment to be the best bodhisattva possible in service to the highest good of all beings, and then I have to let go and let nature unfold in divine timing.

I am so grateful for all the reminders around me – it is not my timing.

Marissa

Marissa and I first met in 2012 when she came to Liberia with her mom who is a "partner forever" in our joint declared passion for supporting women of Africa. Marissa helped us orchestrate the 2nd Annual All Liberian Women's Summit which was a huge success. She fell in love with my namesake Deborah who was four years old at the time, and touched "adopted son" Moses who was 13 in a way he had never opened to conversation and feelings before.

Marissa and her mom, treasured friend Barbara, and I spent the day together today in Coronado, California and then this evening in my home community of La Jolla. At only sixteen years of age, Marissa is one of the oldest souls I have ever been blessed to meet, an amazing teacher for me.

Marissa and her family came to Southern California for a wedding, Marissa's first and a celebration of a 30-year-old friendship for mother Barbara. Marissa met Quinn, the nephew of the bride. OMG! The impact on both of them, and now on me as well as I listen to her speak of Quinn's emotional intelligence, his ability to be present, how he raised the bar for behavior of all boys around her, how their connection is setting the stage for possibilities beyond what she ever imagined – all with no sense of needing to be connected physically as he is in Pasadena, California and she is in Evergreen, Colorado. A deep knowing about joy and possibility had greatly impacted her, and as I assured her, greatly impacted Quinn as well; big learnings are not one-sided.

We finished our special day at a restaurant overlooking the sea. Marissa was beautifully dressed, poised and confident in her skin. She graciously received every compliment or acknowledgment with a sincere *"thank you"* which brought such joy to my heart. I never learned to receive and say just those two words when a compliment came my way until I was nearly 40 years old.

Marissa gave me hope today that the women following me do in fact have the courage to keep the bar high, to not settle for unacceptable as acceptable behavior, to dream of possibilities beyond one's wildest dreams.

Marissa, you are so my teacher and I am so beyond blessed to have you in my life.

The carved stone I bought from the yoga studio today where you and your mom had your massages is engraved with "HOPE" which is what you gave me today Marissa, hope that the paradigm is actually shifting thanks to decades of activism on behalf of women and girls. And hope that no woman anywhere every again will settle for what I have settled for in varying degrees much of my life, abuse by the masculine.

I am so grateful for the learning, late though it is, I have it. And now I am inspired to let Marissa lead the way to a new way of being for the feminine which will heal not only we women but certainly men as well. A major shift is under way which Marissa and her enlightened friends are now leading with my steadfast support. The baton is passing, and gratefully with such confidence after my day with Marissa.

I love you Marissa. My heart is so full of joy after being with you today. Divine Mother is guiding our way. So very glad you and I both believe She is in charge. I am so grateful.

Chapter 8

Liberia

Where are her people?

I awake Christmas morning in a small village in the eastern part of Liberia, twelve hours from the capital of Monrovia over the most astonishingly awful roads I have ever seen or experienced. I make a cup of tea and go outside to sit in a gazebo over-looking the river and watch the canoe water taxi. It is not like any Christmas morning I have ever experienced.

I slowly sip my tea and begin writing in my journal. How did a young girl from the middle of America end up here? People join me in the gazebo. They have conversations with each other. They don't attempt to involve me. I am the only white person in the village and maybe the only white person some of them have ever seen.

After some time Emily joins us all. She starts to explain to the people gathered that I live in a place called California, that I live in a house by myself, that I cook my own food, that I wash my own clothes, that I clean my house, that I drive my own car... I watch the eyes of those gathered get bigger and bigger until one person finally exclaims, *"Well where are her people??"*

A question I have been asking all my life.

They are my people. I have come home.

Perhaps I volunteered to incarnate without a tribe, without a sense of community and belonging? Perhaps I volunteered to bring their story to the rest of the world? Perhaps I am exactly where I need to be for the highest good of all beings, including me? Perhaps Divine Mother is really in charge and it is all good...

Gratitude always.

My Namesake Deborah

In February 2008 I received a phone call from friend Arthur Tamba in Liberia. He said, *"She's here!" "Who's here Arthur?" "Deborah!" "Deborah who?" "Deborah!! She was just born! You can come and get her whenever you want!"*

There is a darling little girl in Liberia named Deborah, my namesake. I am not coming to get her but I am continually coming to see her.

Deborah and I have been connected for six birthdays now. The cards I have delivered for each year are proudly displayed in her house. We have a bond which is beyond words – pure love and pure joy.

As friend Emily in Liberia often says, *"It's a God-thing."* Deborah and I – *it's a God-thing.* How likely is it that the two of us would connect with each other this lifetime among the seven billion people on this planet??

I am so grateful for Deborah and all I am learning from her – unconditional love and endless joy.

Mother Teresa of Liberia

"It's a God-thing" we often say. How did a young girl from Lexington in the far eastern Sinoe County of Liberia and a young girl from the middle of America ever find each other? There is no other explanation – *"It's a God-thing."*

Emily Guegbeh Peal walked into my Foundation for Women office in San Diego at the beginning of 2006, just after the election of President Ellen Johnson Sirleaf, the first female president of an African nation.

Much has happened in the last years of our work together, but nothing like my realization today – Emily is the Mother Teresa of Liberia.

I have witnessed her interaction with our microcredit women for years now, how she speaks their language and inspires and gives hope to them in addition to providing funding for their small businesses. I have witnessed how she honors her family, especially her mother Ma Frances, who is in her nineties and whom she brought back to Liberia with her after years in America as refugees. I have witnessed how she brings children into her home and treats them as her own, children who would have no one and live on the street, and teaches them *"to do right"* while giving them an education. I have witnessed how she interacts with the President, Vice President and leading officials in her country and wins their hearts and respect.

Today I had a new witnessing at a rally for thousands of her fellow country men and women for peace and reconciliation. She is their "Mother," their Mother Teresa. The handicapped men from the war all know her. The poor women all know her. The lost children instinctively all know her. Her people all know her.

I touched her shoulder this afternoon with deep knowing and said *"It is such a blessing that you came home to your country – not just for the women we serve at the Foundation for Women but also for the young women and girls of your country. They need you and your example Emily, the example of an accomplished woman with an education and commitment to service to humanity, and for giving them hope."*

How did I ever get so blessed to be a witness to this? I am beyond grateful to you Divine Mother as I am so clear this is *"A God-thing."*

Moses

On Christmas Day 2006 I awoke for the first time ever in Liberia, West Africa. I had followed my dear colleague Emily Guegbeh Peal from America back to her home where she would live for the first time in nearly 20 years. As has been their long-time family custom, Christmas Day meant opening their home and garden to any child who had nothing special to do on Christmas. There must have been more than 200 children that day. Some were dressed smartly with extra bows and barrettes in their hair. Some were in shorts and t-shirts and barefoot; Moses was in the latter group.

Friend Kevin had his camera to document our first experience in this African nation that was just beginning to heal from years of destruction and senseless war. He recorded a Christmas celebration like no other I had ever experienced with so many special photos. And there showing up over and over again was Moses. His smile was infectious; his joy compelling despite his circumstances.

At the end of a most special day I said to friend Emily, *"If you can find Moses, I will pay for him to go to school."* She did find him and Moses started going to school for the first time as an 8-year-old. Gratefully his parents came to Emily after a few months asking if Moses could stay with her on the weekends as they were illiterate and unable to help him with his school work. And before too long there was another request from them, could Moses please stay all the time, *"You better just take him."*

Moses drew a picture for me a couple of years ago. It was of a young boy with a village on one side and a house like Emily's on the other. The boy in the center was crying. We have talked about that drawing several times since he gave it to me. Moses is now in the 8th grade and was a winning contestant in the recent National Spelling Bee. He is so smart and so grateful for all the opportunities that have appeared since that Christmas morning when he just kept showing up in Kevin's camera. And he misses his birth family and…

I am very grateful for the dear connection Moses and I have; he is truly my son. I chose as a child not to be a biological mother this life time. Divine Mother has since blessed me with connections to many children this lifetime. Moses stands out from them all – just as he did that first Christmas morning in Liberia.

I pray that our connection since that Christmas Day is for the highest good for Moses and all… So grateful and blessed by our connection Moses. I love you.

A Call from Liberia

I received a call from Liberia today from a friend visiting there. *"I am so tired! I am just back from 10 hours of being gone. After the party yesterday! I have to lie down."*

Remarkable.

Only later in the conversation did I hear and find out, *"I was in the car with the Vice President and the Second Lady and Head of Security Arthur – just the four of us – zooming past all the traffic pulled over on the side of the road for us." "I was introduced by the VP as his nephew to the crowd of hundreds." "I met the President Pro Tem of the Senate and several other dignitaries."*

Gratitude was so missing in this conversation despite the unbelievable circumstances that only a handful of people might ever experience. Work in Liberia is not easy, especially for those of us from the US; those of us who can always go home to the comforts of our life outside of Africa, outside of this totally war-torn and wrecked country.

Always gratitude frames everything and every moment for me. I am very grateful for the reminder – always a choice to choose gratitude which was so missing from this conversation.

Hot shower and warm food...

I was so blessed today to attend the *"Peace + Reconciliation = 1 Liberia Jamboree"* in Monrovia with two Nobel Peace Prize Laureates, President Ellen Johnson Sirleaf and Leymah Gbowee, and thousands of Liberian people, dignitaries, committed peace activists and some with other agendas…

It was a very hot and sunny day. At a sandy field in downtown Monrovia with no shade for the masses – and I might add, no bathrooms or drinking water – I sat in the shade under an umbrella as a special guest, my feet on a carpet and my bottom in a plastic chair the back of which said *"Thank God".*

Yes, I was far from the comforts of the developed world – witnessing history in the making as war was being left behind finally for peace in this small West African nation – celebrating the re-election of the first female president on the continent. And it was all made easy for me to be a witness today. I had a driver to and from the event, a chair in the shade a few seats away from President Ellen and Leymah, a gifted t-shirt and wrist band, a front row view of the celebration. All without asking.

I came home from the event at the end of the afternoon, took a hot shower to wash away my sweat and dirt and then filled my belly with warm rice and vegetables. And I am wondering how many of the thousands today who were so happy to celebrate peace and "their Special Ma" (President Ellen) are still finding their way home by walking as I write this? And to what are they headed? What will their day be like tomorrow? And their next day and their next day as they get up every day trying to survive in this totally war-torn physically wrecked country?

I know that I am part of 20% of the population that shares more than 90% of the wealth. I am so trying to do something about changing the statistics of poverty. Today that gap between my reality and the reality of 90% of the people of this country showed up in a very amazing way.

I came home to a hot shower and warm food. And they? I am beyond grateful – and so committed to change this reality so all of us can be grateful.

Koffa

I have learned so much from people who live outside of the 20% of us that consume more than 90% of the earth's resources and wealth.

Koffa Toe is my friend. Today I asked him to please clone himself so there could be a Koffa in America as well as in Liberia. He did not know the word "clone." Now he does, and I know he wishes he could do that very thing, clone himself and come to America – to be of service to me and the Foundation for Women; his own benefit being his second thought I am certain.

Koffa is our Foundation for Women Liberia driver. He makes a fortune in this war-torn ravaged country – almost $4/day – and with that he supports himself and his family, being his wife and three daughters. $125 a month for housing and food and school fees and clothes and fun and hope – beyond my comprehension.

Koffa shows up for work every day dressed in a perfectly pressed shirt and a special tie – immaculate in every way. He is meticulous with his driving records and the vehicle.

Koffa is one of my life heroes. He drives through the most impossible situations imaginable with determination and skill and commitment to deliver his passengers safely – and with patience and trust.

Patience and trust have been my life lessons and learning. Koffa is one of my greatest teachers and I am beyond grateful for him, for knowing him, for the service he extends to me, for the joy he brings to me.

So grateful for you Koffa!

Big people versus little people

I called the Vice President of Liberia today at 2:00PM here in Liberia. I had called earlier in the day to let him know that I had arrived after a long delay due to airline mechanical issues and was sorry to miss our scheduled meeting for the previous day. This time he took my call immediately. We exchanged our familiar *"HEY FABULOUS!"* greetings to each other, something that has become our dear name for each other.

After our hello, I mentioned that there was a problem with a visa for a dear supporter of our work whom he knows, Ann, and that her daughter was at that moment in front of someone at the Liberian Consulate in DC asking for an immediate visa renewal . The VP listened when I said that I had been trying to call his staff since arriving 18 hours earlier and no one would answer their phone.

"That's the difference between the big people and the little people," he said. *"The big people don't answer their phone; the little people always answer their phone. I am a little people."*

"I am so glad to be in your wonderful little people company Sir!" was my reply.

He soon called back to say that the needed visa was in Ann's passport and all was OK. The Vice President of a country had called me personally to say an issue I had tried to get his staff to resolve was now fixed and he wanted to let me know personally. Little people talking to each other.

We are both little people and we know it. We love and care about each other and all beings. We answer our phones and we make things happen. We love being little people in a big world – making miracles happen every day for people.

I am beyond grateful for the company of little people with whom I keep doing beyond big things in the world – thank you dearest VP, treasured friend.

Monrovia, Liberia

I sat by the sea today – twice. I sat. I breathed in and out. I mindfully watched the waves coming into the beach. I wondered. And I wrote.

It is a defining moment in my life, here in Liberia. I need and want your help Divine Mother and Angels.

A lifetime pattern is now so clear, a pattern from childhood . My dealing with and coping with the pain has always been present: hurry, fix it, make it better and numbing to sooth it.

I understand and am intimate with pain and suffering; it is my life experience.

Relief came as I wrote today by the sea.

I have been reading and writing and wondering for more than 60 years now. Will it all ever make sense??

I am grateful for my journal and grateful for this time by the sea… Truth appeared.

Ma Frances

I missed a call in the middle of the night from Liberia. Ma Frances was calling on Mother's Day there to let me know how loved I am – pure joy for me! Then I awoke this morning to find a fabulous text message from her. God sent me a very special gift this life time – Ma Frances.

Ma Frances just celebrated her 94th birthday. She lives in Liberia where the average life expectancy is half that age. How is this possible?? She is pure love. It is so wonderfully easy to see the Divine in Ma Frances as she so easily sees the Divine in all beings. She is my inspiration.

We all need heroes. I have been blessed this lifetime to have been connected to many inspiring women, older women who I have so admired and appreciated. The biological women in my family of birth were not role models for me. For the most, they modeled worry and fear, a way of being which I knew at an early age was not how I wanted to live.

Ma Frances is my super hero. Her life story is filled with surprises. She left her first husband soon after their marriage as he expected her to stay home and take care of the children and the home, nothing more. That did not work for her. She married again and raised her children in the small village of Lexington in eastern Sinoe County, a community of few hundred people where she was the community teacher for 40 years. Her belief and trust in God has pervaded everything in her life; deep unwavering faith.

Ma Frances, daughter Emily and son-in-law Alex are now raising the 51st and 52nd children who are not theirs biologically. Moses who is 15 and so smart first appeared six years ago. He had never been to school and was selling water in the streets to help support his family. Decontee is 13 and appeared a couple of years ago when her biological family discarded her as they thought she was a witch. It makes me believe in a bigger plan as these two children have become beyond dear to me. And now Amelia has come… They just keep coming to this haven of love headed by Ma Frances.

I am so grateful for Ma Frances and her presence in my life and in this world. I want to grow up and be just like her – total love, total peace, total trust, total service despite living in a totally wrecked country with no postman and no green salads. After returning to Liberia from years in America as a refuge, Ma Frances misses these two favorite things the most.

I am beyond grateful for this amazing role model in my life – tremendous love and great gratitude to you Ma Frances.

PS On Thanksgiving Day in America in 2013, I spent several hours with Ma Frances at her home in Monrovia, Liberia – first with her at her breakfast table and then in comfy chairs in the living room. She read this story about her from my computer without needing glasses and then the one about her daughter Emily. She is happy to be in my book and amazed by the love she has in her life, "Plenty-O" as she says in Liberian English with a smile.

I learned that her name is really spelled Francess with an emphasis on the "cess" – I said, "As in princess!" Her Pa named her and so loved her.

We talked about her first 94 years, her up-coming 95th birthday, and both marveled at the fact she is still alive. I said, "It is because you are pure love and give it to everyone." And she replied, "I do love everyone." I mentioned a spiritual book I had just read which speaks of the levels of love from love that comes from the lower chakra energy centers and is all about self-gratification to the higher evolved love which extends out to all beings which is where Ma Frances lives. She smiled softly.

She now calls daughter Emily "Momma" and wonders why. She needs help with many of her physical needs and surrenders with grace.

We held hands for a long time in silence before she finally agreed to a nap.

This is the greatest Thanksgiving Day of my life ever Ma Frances – thank you – I love you more than words can say.

Beyond Imaginable...

It is early 2014 and I am in Liberia, my fourth trip here in the last 10 months. My last visit ended December 15, 2013 and I had no plans to return so quickly – until our major education partner decided to return to Liberia the last week in January and a special donor expressed an interest to come after visiting a project in Rwanda. So I arranged to return after just a short time back in the US to welcome them.

I planned to stay in Liberia for a few weeks after our guests departed; thinking I might investigate opportunities for spending more time here, perhaps find alternative living arrangements to the hotel, investigate possible business opportunities to raise funds for the Foundation for Women Liberia microfinance work, spend more time with the numerous children I love and sponsor here…

Instead I have become witness to one of the saddest experiences of my life. I have watched my dearest sister and colleague exhibit unbelievably behavior. She has refused to travel to the US for medical treatment after suffering a stroke in Liberia December 5th. Now months later and without proper medical care, a torrent of rage has been un-leased and I have become the target. My life is in danger.

Just when I thought it could not get worse, I discovered late one Sunday evening that dear "son" Moses to whom I have been connected since Christmas 2006 was arrested early that morning after being accused of stealing a television out of the home where I have sponsored him to be for years. I orchestrated his stay in the home of my trusted colleague and have been paying his school fees since 2007. He had never been to school when we first met and now he is the top student in his 8th grade class.

My colleague and her husband had a Medicine Man come to the house about the missing TV. They asked if Moses stole their television and he confirmed yes by putting a nut into Moses' palm, which then turned "warm"; Moses felt no warmth. On that word, the police came, handcuffed Moses, and took him to jail.

Moses' friends alerted me to his circumstances Sunday evening. I was advised by the VP's head of security to let it be for the night; that my intervention might be harmful for Moses.

The thought of him spending the night in jail tormented me. On Monday I spoke with a Liberian attorney and learned that it is illegal to hold a 15-year-old child in jail. I called a judge I knew in the judicial system and his intervention resulted in Moses' release within an hour. He was released to a Liberian man who works for a colleague – no questions asked as to whom or why, so my participation is known to no one at the jail and hopefully not to anyone else. Moses is safe and will never return to what I thought was a wonderful home.

I have learned that my former colleague paid the police money to come and arrest Moses and that she was at the jail Monday morning with more money to make sure he stayed in jail.

What would have happened to Moses if I had not come and stayed? What might have happened to the Foundation for Women if I had not listened to you Divine Mother and returned?

I have a sense that my life is in danger. Whoever would have thought? I adopted this country and the special people of Liberia my first trip here in December 2006. It has become my home and its people have become my family. And now the beyond imaginable has occurred.

I am filled with gratitude that I was here in Liberia to be in all these conversations; to save the Foundation for Women work from ending; and to intervene on behalf of Moses. I trust you Divine Mother completely that my steps are being guided – that I am not walking through all this by myself – that there is goodness and light at the end of this challenge.

Complete and Utter Disappointment

The Vice President of Liberia is a very wise and calm-mannered man. I have never seen him agitated since first meeting him in 2006. I have learned much from him over the many years of our special friendship.

"In any situation Deborah, I make a list of all possible outcomes and Complete and Utter Disappointment is always on the list. Then if that occurs I am not surprised."

The VP shared this wisdom with me in 2013 when someone we thought was a dear friend to both of us and the country of Liberia abruptly decided to pursue a very different path and walked away. It was a painful time. I did, however, take comfort in the Vice President's words of wisdom – Complete and Utter Disappointment is always a possible outcome in any situation.

Here I am in Liberia in early 2014 once again having a conversation with the VP about Complete and Utter Disappointment, this time regarding my dear colleague, sister and head of the Foundation for Women's work in Liberia for the last seven years. The unimaginable has occurred – mismanagement of donor funding, fraud and perhaps criminal behavior. *"In any situation Deborah, Complete and Utter Disappointment is always a possible outcome."*

Surprisingly I am now peaceful in that knowing, and in the knowing that this is Divine Mother's work in Liberia, not mine. My job is to continue to trust completely and to dedicate all of my actions to the highest good of all beings again and again.

I believe that every behavior comes from love or fear. My colleague's behavior is a cry for help coming from a place of tremendous fear. I am not matching that energy. Instead I am sending love and gratitude. And doing the meditation practice of tonglen – breathing in her pain and breathing out love back to her. And trusting Divine Mother completely; all is unfolding just as it needs to…

I am grateful for this major learning. I can be in peace in the midst of Complete and Utter Disappointment.

A Shift in Liberia

Exhausted by sadness, stress, grief and wonderment, I took a shower and went to bed just after sunset on Valentine's Day as so many were just beginning their celebration of love and joy. I slept for 10 hours, possibly the first real sleep I have had in weeks. It has not been easy living in a compound with guards watching out for my safety and checking on me outside my bedroom door throughout the night for days.

Awakening well before dawn, I called my spiritual teacher in the US for a reality check-in. All I knew and am feeling is indeed true; my physical safety is of the highest priority. I finished the call relieved for her love on the other end of the line and the calmness of her voice despite the circumstances here in Liberia.

I prepared for my morning meditation – and then began to sit quietly; first noticing my breath coming in and out as I peacefully settled into a familiar place of deep rest. Then I began tonglen practice once again – picturing dear former colleague and her divine nature seated in front of me; I began to breathe in her fear and anger and breathe out love in return to her. I have been committed to this practice daily, several times a day, since the crisis began weeks ago.

I ended my practice with a loving-kindness practice for her and all concerned by the events in Liberia – May all beings be free from worry and fear, may all beings be safe, may all beings be filled with a sense of well-being, may all beings be surrounded by loving-kindness and compassion. And then my daily prayer conversation with Divine Mother.

When my meditation was complete, I quietly opened my eyes and noticed. I felt a shift; a major shift. There was no more emotion – sadness, stress, grief or wonderment. I was somehow elevated above it all and now a silent observer. And there was more, much more. I had the deep knowing that this present bodhisattva assignment was almost complete; that what I volunteered to do with her for the last eight years was about to be finished; that all the experiences in my life have been assignments for which I volunteered – in service to the highest good of all beings, including me, by helping to bring light to darkness.

Staggering knowing and total peace. I sat with it, wrote in my journal about it, went outside to the sea with it. The knowing and the peace remain. I have been journaling my feelings all day. Smiling, my only request is that I have some rest before my next big assignment… My heart is bursting with gratitude Divine Mother.

Chapter 9

Choice

Bowing in gratitude

After years I find myself back in Thailand – and my heart is bursting with joy! My work has taken me to Africa for the last decade. Now I am remembering why I feel so at home in Asia, particularly in Thailand. In a previous work life, I spent more than a decade in Asia much of my time. It holds a dear and special place in my heart.

The people of this special country are deeply connected to their spiritual life. There is no separation between life and spiritual practice – it is one and the same always. Each greeting is made with hands together in front of the heart – Namaste – always with a bow to acknowledge the Divine in each other.

Yesterday after having a Thai massage, I wrote in my journal that certainly being back here now is a gift, is part of my spiritual practice and not just to chair a breakout session at the Rotary Convention. I have been practicing seeing the Divine in all beings always, trying to release all judgments and opinions. I am reminded why this is a spiritual practice because I must practice mindfully every moment to continually see the Divine in all beings – something which appears to come so very easily to the people of Thailand. Being in this place where the Divine is so present is pure bliss.

We are delayed in leaving Bangkok for India due to visa issues for my Liberian colleagues. Unfortunate or fortunate? Trust and patience – my life lessons showing up again. Somehow it all seems just as it needs to be with more time here. I am so grateful.

Trust and Patience

I keep coming back to trust and patience.

I don't know what is best for me, for anyone else, for the world. I am on the path, committed to my own enlightenment for the benefit of all living beings.

And everything brings me back to trust and patience.

When I was a child I prayed every night to God to *"please get me out of here."* I knew I did not fit with these people or in this place. I knew I belonged somewhere else.

"Star light, star bright, first star I see tonight. I wish I may, I wish I might, have this wish I wish tonight – Please get me out of here!"

For years I prayed this same prayer, and for years I stayed right where I was. And then when I finally graduated from high school, I left to go to college beginning a few days later. Trust and patience. All in divine timing instead of my own timing.

It took me years to find my true spiritual practice. In a metaphysical bookstore while in my early adult life, I found John Bradshaw's *"The Family"* and read to my amazement that there were others with feelings as I had had my whole life; that there are patterns, rules and attitudes in families passed from one generation to another that lead to 96% of all families being emotionally impaired to some degree. Such relief. I wasn't an alien from another planet. I was a product of dysfunction and I was determined to find wholeness.

I have kept coming back to trust and patience ever since that awareness. I am committed to doing all I can do to stay in a place of wholeness instead of perpetuating dysfunction. And I can only stay there with trust and patience. So grateful.

An Unexpected Visitor

I was spending a quiet Sunday in the astonishing spiritual sanctuary that I am blessed to call home – sitting on the patio by the sea, reading *"The Gift"* by Hafiz, *"The Big Leap"* by Hendricks and writing in my ever present journal…

When YIKES! a squirrel came up the stairs leading to my sanctuary and went right into my home!

My reaction was immediate – *NO!* Then a pause and a question to myself, *"Can I always come from a place of love vs fear?"* Quite a time to see…

I came into my home, closed doors leading to other rooms so my guest could only be in the living/dining space and the kitchen. I waited for a moment in the entry and then from love, knowing he did not want to be in my home any more than I wanted him to be there, I walked with knowing into the living room and lovingly declared, *"You are just going to have to leave the way you came in."* And within seconds he departed – out to the patio – down the stairs and off to another adventure.

It was a first of its kind experience in almost two decades of having this spot by the sea.

I drew an angel card from my special box later in the afternoon, something I had not done for some time. The message read: *"NOTICE THE SIGNS" "Yes, the signs you've been receiving are heaven-sent. We drop feathers, coins and other signs upon your path to remind you that you're loved and never alone."*

Now I know that the squirrel was a "she" – and she was a dramatic part of that angel card message. She got my attention. And I am so grateful for the reframe – and the reinforcement of the knowing that I am loved and never alone…

Today

My mindfulness thought for the day is *"When faced with a feeling of stagnation and confusion, it may be helpful to take an hour, an afternoon, or even several days to reflect on what it is that will truly bring us happiness."*

I am sitting alone by the sea reflecting and wondering. Am I blessed by all my experiences, all the pain, all the hurt, all the sadness? Is everyone truly behaving exactly the way they need to in order to contribute to my enlightenment? Can I really surround everything with loving-kindness and compassion? Can I surround myself with loving-kindness and compassion?

I believe that I signed up for big lessons this life time, that I have had experiences so I can deeply "know" from a cellular level. My gratitude list is long. Yet I am sobbing with sadness this morning – tired of being alone so much of this life, tired of not fitting in, tired... and grateful to be writing... gratitude always.

It takes a commitment to always find gratitude...

The BIG WAVE hit this morning – unexpectedly, powerfully, unceasing. Down – tried to get up. Down again – and again – and again.

A phone call from Africa woke me up. It was early-afternoon there, before dawn in California, and I was suddenly and surprisingly awake – all I wanted was to go back to sleep in the safety of my fetal position under the mountains of covers. My sense of safety was interrupted and gone.

And then the wave of constant tears – deep loneliness, aching for a family I have never experienced, waves and mountains of sadness and grief that did not stop for hours.

My dear friend Janie and I had a telephone call scheduled for noon. I thought I could be present in my suck-it-up-manner as I always do. No. I heard her dear voice say *"How are you?"* and I went to my place of reality – sobs of sorrow and pain.

How much is in there? When will I be able to release it all? This time?

Janie and I share a similar reality. Our bond was cemented after almost a decade of connection when we spent time together one afternoon in her spiritual sanctuary in Santa Fe. We had known each other for years but had never spoken our truths to each other: *"I could never be your friend as you were the leader of a global movement to end poverty for women and girls." "I could never be your friend as you held a high place of spiritual commitment and being that I could only aspire to."* We sat in her hacienda courtyard in the sunshine before the fire in the corner of her space and spoke our truths to each other.

And we spoke of the waves of grief that keep coming up for both of us – how at this stage in our lives we do not, as Janie says, *"have a soft spot to land."* Neither of us ever expected to not have a life partner.

So when we connected by phone that Saturday, I spoke my truth to her immediately knowing that we share a place of deep trust and knowing and respect, *"A big wave is overtaking me,"* I said. I told her of sharing my truth and the Foundation for Women reality in a special circle at our FFW Center the previous Wednesday.   Repeating the history of the last months of betrayal and sadness made it all real; no more denial. Then I told her of going to a special TED event Friday evening by myself, driving home by myself, having an epiphany by myself – I am so done with being by myself.   We have both been missing that soft spot to land.

But we do in reality have such a place. We have Divine Mother. And She provides the softest possible place to land. I know that now. That Saturday all I wanted was a lifeguard to protect me from the pounding big wave. And you sent me one – dear Janie.

It is not always easy, this practice of always finding gratitude. But it is my committed practice. Gratitude always.

What if it is all Divinely Ideal?

I am blessed to have the gift of years. So many experiences. So many travels all over the world. So many different living situations.

I did not follow the model of my birth family in the middle of America. I did not have 2.4 children, a double car garage and a dog. I did not set up a savings fund for children's college education at their birth; I did not have children. I did not "fit in" in any way from the time I arrived to this incarnation – and knew it from the earliest age.

And what if that is exactly what was supposed to happen? Was I supposed to go off to Boulder, Colorado to college at the end of the 1960s? Was I supposed to marry young to help keep a friend out of going to Vietnam during that war? Was I supposed to find my way to California from, for me, the oppressive Midwest of America? Was I supposed to start an international financial research company with my last husband and see the world as I never imagined? Was I supposed to birth the Foundation for Women in support of women whose voices are not heard as mine had so not been heard my entire life? Was I supposed to connect with Deveraj in India and Suresh in Zambia and Lynn in South Africa and Barbro in Niger – and ultimately Emily in Liberia? Was I supposed to experience betrayal as I could never imagine, especially by women who I so trusted had my back? Was I supposed to experience betrayal by my life partner, best friend and lover? Was I supposed to experience the near death of the organization I birthed; and consequently the leaving of my spiritual sanctuary by the sea where I thought I would be forever? Was I supposed to land in a small cottage in my treasured community where a male intruder appeared, standing in my new living room in the darkness of night just days after I arrived one evening?

What if it is all divinely ideal?

I am surveying the main cottage room now as I write this and see such great joy - in the four-foot doll from South Africa I carried home more than a decade ago; in my beloved Buddha from Hong Kong who chose me three decades ago; in the beautiful orchid with white angel wings; in the thangka from Nepal, in "Joyce" who is from a doll project in South Africa that was a sell-out hit at Sotherby's in London; in the walking stick from the Masai in Kenya when I was there and first met artist Kioko who is now a dear friend; in the framed 8X10 photo of a woman in Liberia with her Foundation for Women t-shirt counting her first loan of L$7000 (US$100) – more money than she has ever seen in her life; in a framed photo of His Holiness the Dalai Lama who just turned 78 with a carved stone I have had for years in front of his photo expressing *"My Religion is Kindness;"* – and in the candles and mindfulness bowls. I/We have created a spiritual sanctuary – again – thank you Divine Mother . So grateful.

I now deeply know that it all is divinely ideal and you Divine Mother have been holding my hand every moment of this incarnation through necessary lessons and learnings and now to total trust. I am so blessed and so filled with gratitude.

I am married to me and my spiritual practice...

I had a conversation today with a woman I have never met. We were connected by a common friend – and I mostly listened … *"I was engaged to a big-shot Silicon Valley guy – my job was to support him. Why? Why is my self-esteem and reality tied to a man?"*

This is our time – time for women to step up in gratitude for all we do.

Several months ago I put three special rings on my ring finger of my left hand, rings I had collected while traveling around the world. I had not worn them for years. Now almost twenty years divorced, I am making my way as a woman of the world without a man next to me.

I have made my way without a marriage and life partnership. I have made my way committed to service to the highest good of all beings with the support of you Divine Mother and so many angels.

The rings I collected while traveling around the world a lifetime ago are now back on my left ring finger. I am so beyond happy to be married to those special memories which brought such joy to me and my heart – and to be OK with just me.

Such gratitude always.

Sufficiency vs scarcity

I grew up in scarcity – there was always just enough but never really enough at the same time. My very young parents had five daughters in just more than six years, thinking that would be better for us and them. Instead yikes! There were so many needs with so many of us and so far to stretch the limited resources. I felt poor, physically, emotionally and spiritually.

Now after years working in microfinance and global development, I understand the difference between scarcity and sufficiency – it is all in one's attitude. My dear Liberian colleague Emily Guegbeh Peal recently gave a TEDxWomen talk in Washington DC where she shared that she *"grew up in poverty and then had plenty; the war in my country took everything and as a refugee in America I again grew to have plenty; I decided to have less when I returned to Liberia after the war so in fact to have more."*

I have spent much time in Liberia the last many years, a country where 85% of the population lives on less than $1/day. And where there is always a choice in attitude between sufficiency and scarcity. I am continually in awe of all who do so much with so little – and with such joy. As Lynne Twist so wonderfully expresses in her classic book *"The Soul of Money," "The life you live is the legacy you leave."* It is always possible to focus on enough – we always have the opportunity to choose our attitude.

There have been many times in my life where money was a concern, where scarcity and fear dominated my thinking. Today in Liberia I have made the commitment to live in sufficiency always. My gratitude list is so long – always sufficiency instead of scarcity, always gratitude.

The Land of Joy

After decades of living in The Land of Abuse, I have made my way with Divine Mother's guidance to The Land of Joy.

It is a new and unfamiliar place this life time, yet there is a deep knowing that I have been here before. I am exhausted by the journey and all the accumulated experiences and lessons that have brought me here. And there is a softness, a release of struggle that is so present and so welcome.

I have left my head and have landed in my heart. There is nothing to figure out here; nothing to make sense of – just a being-ness in my commitment to my true bodhisattva nature. And a total trust in Divine Mother.

I have left so many people behind on this journey – not good or bad; just a fact. Everyone is doing the best they can at every given moment. All is sacred and holy and divinely ideal. I miss many and at the same time I have excitement about the many I will now meet in this new land.

I am being present with the transition, resting from the journey. I do look back and wonder how people who were so dear to me are doing. The losses this lifetime have been many; intellectually I know necessary but emotionally, wonderment is present. I am being with the wonderment, trusting that all is divinely ideal. And I am resting for the next part of this journey with a deep knowing that it will be very different here in The Land of Joy than where I have been…

I am feeling beyond blessed to be here and filled with tremendous gratitude – thank you Divine Mother.

Chapter 10

Finding My Voice

It was like a normal day...

Instead of quiet time with coffee/tea and beyond special conversation together to begin the day, I now have quiet with me and the sea each morning – mindful of how different my life has become within just a matter of days.

Gratitude – such gratitude – for the greatest learning and lesson of my life. It all started when I was a child, being chosen by my father as his psychological and emotional partner. My life ever since has been trying to make sense of it all always. Now I've got it – the big life lesson – all so very clear. Yikes – so very big.

I have spent a life time trying to make people do, be and feel what they do not want to do, be and feel. I have spent a life time trying to make unavailable people like my father available. I have tried to find love from people who are not available to give it. And in the meantime, I have driven myself and them crazy. I surrender.

My gratitude is deep and genuine, my understanding profound and my relief enormous.

Now that I have quiet time by myself next to the sea each morning, I – like poet David Whyte who so wisely learned and chose this quiet time each day – am present with the morning without doing, making it a *"prelude to possibility rather than something that frightens me back into the same corner I left just the previous day."* Instead of getting out the door to exercise after checking my computer and iphone immediately upon awakening, I sit in silence with my favorite candle. We, me and the sea, welcome the day in quiet before I am called "to do" – such a new and wonderful practice.

And then today I read something that so reminded me of him, my spirit partner. I sent a text about page 84 of *"Anam Cara"* – and heard back. And then a phone call from him at noon – and another at 4PM with an offer of help for my work, again... It felt like a normal day. Regular days are/were filled with connections with my best friend, lover and partner.

But there is a new normal now. He needs his space, he says without a relationship – and truly I need mine. He had the courage I did not have to speak the truth – the chaos of life was not supporting either of us. But until I understood the final piece in my life learning, I did not have the courage to say good bye. So he did and pushed me into my final knowing – supposedly for his own need, really a great gift to me.

Then today was like normal – regular connections and conversations and offers of support… I loved and relished it all, until I remembered that the normal of then is not the normal of now. I called and reminded him – it cannot be both ways. Your requested time-out eliminates our normal social connections and our previous, yes precious so much of the time, normal is finished, awaiting what will be next… Taking care of me while honoring and accepting his request at the same time is what I am committed to do. May we both find a way to keep turning into the conversation as we go forward separately until what is next becomes clear.

Trying to find a new normal is not easy.

Gratitude and love always…

An Intruder and My Scream

I moved from my treasured spiritual sanctuary by the sea in June – a total surprise. After months of loss and sadness and turmoil, I was drawn to the cottage, a short distance from dear mentor Murray's house – I was divinely led is the truth.

I was just starting to energetically arrive after being in the cottage for two weeks, when at 3 AM in the morning an intruder opened the kitchen window over the sink and entered. I had not been sleeping well that evening as the day had been an extremely emotional one after yet another major loss in a string of losses over many months. I had been up writing in my journal in the living room at 1 AM – and had left my journal and treasured crystal pendulum on the sofa.

Just a short time later, I awoke to a presence in the cottage. At first I thought it was the energy of the elderly woman who had recently vacated; she had left crying with sadness. Then it became very clear that someone was truly in my new cottage space – grabbing a bathrobe, I jumped from bed and screamed like I have never screamed in my life! I continued to scream and scream and scream as I reached for the phone to call 911. The intruder left through the kitchen door breaking everything in his path. The 911 operator held me in an embrace of safety as I sobbed hysterically and waited for the police.

Incredible trauma and violation. My tremendously powerful scream ended what could have been so much worse. And my scream was about so much more than the intruder – I found a huge voice of rage inside of me I never knew I had. NO MORE! I screamed out not just the intruder but my recently betraying partner, the betraying Foundation for Women "J Team" members, all from whom I have accepted abuse over decades as I so thought it was all I deserved. NO MORE!

I am grateful for the intruder – and pray for his peace and well-being. He took my treasured crystal pendulum, my special healing gift to him. He gave me a special gift; I found a huge voice inside of me I had never experienced – DONE WITH ABUSE! I became the voice for all women everywhere – DONE WITH ABUSE!

With great gratitude whoever you are Intruder; gratitude always.

Truth Be Told

I am in my sixties – how did that happen?

Another series of events has caused me once again to do a life review. I made a request of Divine Mother that this might be another new beginning – but for the last time, please. Then I quickly remembered that I am not in charge and surrendered. I will take as many new beginnings as come my way.

I am in my spiritual sanctuary by the sea which I will attempt to refinance once again, this time to eliminate the debt left behind when three women I trusted with my life followed a donor I once believed to be a gift from the heavens to begin a non-profit separate from the Foundation for Women. Yikes – paralysis for six months due to sheer disbelief.

But the truth be told, I have experienced so many circumstances which did not support me since childhood. I came to believe at an early age that I should not have been born, that I was a terrible example for my younger sisters, that what came out of my mouth was so awful that it needed to be cleaned with a bar of soap regularly.

So in a life review at sunset this evening sitting amidst the greatest betrayal and financial challenge of my life, I am reviewing… how I never fit as a child, how I gave my virginity away without realizing what was happening once I left home for college (don't talk, don't think, don't feel were the unstated rules of the house while I was growing up), how I settled for unavailable men in order to be loved and feel a part of something though all the while feeling like an alien, how again and again that pattern has presented itself in my life – culminating now in the possible demise of 20 years of a foundation I birthed to support women whose voices are not heard, just like my own so much of my life.

The truth be told, I cannot continue this pattern any longer. I am done with it. And I am grateful, so grateful. Appearing as if all is beyond wonderful – winning award after award, while aching inside with loneliness – that reality is over today. The truth be told from this moment forward.

I am a champion for women whose voices are not heard as I am one of them.

I am a champion for women who do not have financial security as I am one of them.

I am a champion for women who continually compromise to feel okay as I am one of them.

I am a champion for women who settle for the crumbs in the kitchen when there is a banquet in the next room as I am one of them.

I am a champion for women who accept the behavior of unavailable people, especially men, thinking that is all there is as I am one of them.

I am a champion for women who get up and do what needs to be done despite all odds as I am one of them.

I am a champion for women who crawl in bed alone at night and wake up alone in the morning and put trust in Divine Mother despite the challenges as I am one of them.

And I am a champion for women everywhere who dream of a different reality as I am one of them.

The truth be told. I am a recognized leader in the global movement in support of women and girls. I am a recognized leader in the global movement to eliminate poverty, especially for women and girls. I am a recognized leader in the philanthropic community – a member of Women Moving Millions, a community committed to raising unprecedented resources for women and girls. I have contributed unprecedented resources to funding the Foundation for Women for the last two decades.

And today, truth be told, I am feeling as I did as a young girl – disconnected and alone and wondering what this life adventure is all about. Is my contribution as a committed bodhisattva making any difference at all? Will I ever feel connected? Will it all ever make sense? Will I ever feel truly a part of some collective entity that is really making a difference for humanity? Will the tears of my reality turn one day into tears of joy?

I am awake. I have surrendered every day, for more than 35 years now, asking Divine Mother please that all my thoughts and words and actions each day may be for the highest good of all beings, including me. I commit to living one day, one moment at a time, each day.

The truth be told that after more than 13,000 daily surrenderings, I am never giving up despite whatever circumstances come my way this lifetime. JOY(CE) recently became part of my spiritual tribe. She is the most wonderful beaded four foot tall doll made by Nthabiseng Maseau-Xhosa, an artist in South Africa in 1992. Joyce is my inspiration daily now. I will just keep being and doing every moment for the highest good for all beings, especially women and girls – including me.

It is time to write a new chapter. I am grateful – always. Today is a new beginning as so well stated in this affirmation prayer from *"Creative Ideas"* –

TODAY IS A NEW BEGINNING

"…I create new heavens and a new earth… Isaiah 65:17

Nothing is ever twice alike. Everything is continuously being re-created, and it literally is true that the creative Spirit is forever making all things new. We must permit It to make them new for us.

I live today as though the words of this my affirmative prayer were already accomplished facts in my experience. I empty my mind of every fear and doubt. I condemn no one and no thing, not even myself. I forget that which is past and have no fear of the future.

I live in harmony with people and with all situations that surround me. I see and feel the presence of good running through everything. I have complete faith that this divine presence reveals itself to me in my every thought, every word, and every act.

There is nothing in my thought about the past or the future that can in any way deny me the pleasure and privilege of living today as though everything was complete and perfect. My whole expectancy is of much and more, of good and better.

The future is bright with hope and fulfillment. The present is perfect, and no past failure mars today's understanding. Today is the start of my new and more successful experience of achievement. And so it is."

I am so thankful for this daily reminder. Thank you dear friend Barbara for sharing this with me. This is the biggest time of change ever in my life. I trust that Divine Mother is in charge. I am so grateful.

On the Other Side of Abuse

My scream came from the deepest part of my being – such astonishing rage that I surprised myself! And it would not stop!

Now that the trauma of the moment is over, the intruder is gone, the cottage is secure, and I have had support from my spiritual teacher, I realize it was all divinely ideal. I have accepted abuse in varying forms my entire life. I was powerless to stop it when I was a child. As an adult I knew it as normal behavior, what I had become so accustomed to – my normal.

Now after my primal scream I see abuse for what it is – so beyond awful! Behavior coming from darkness instead of light. A dishonoring of all souls involved, the abuser and the abused. And not how Spirit intended all created light beings to be with each other.

Now that I have found my deepest voice, my deepest and boldest and strongest – NO MORE! I am full of feelings of gratitude and sadness. I am so grateful that I found my voice in such a powerful way. I am so glad that I awoke to the intruder and could scream my NO MORE!

And I am so very sad for my years of not having a powerful voice in response to behaviors that were not supportive of me. I am sad for the intruder and his need to behave in such a manner. I am sad for all the people I screamed out of my life along with the intruder, so many who under the guise of offering love instead offered abuse from my infancy for decades. I pray for all of them – for their peace and well-being and enlightenment to a very different way of being.

I am on the other side – never again will I be in relationship where integrity and love and kindness and respect are not fully present within and present for all involved. I am so very grateful for this amazing life lesson – so grateful to be on the other side of abuse, so grateful for Divine Mother's hand in guiding me to this new place.

A completely new life I could never have imagined is possible now…
Tremendous gratitude.

Chapter 11

Divine Mother

My Daily Prayer

My spiritual practice is the most important part of my life. My daily conversation with God and all Enlightened Beings helping me has evolved over years of Al-Anon and Buddhist practices and yoga and biblio-therapy and more.

An Al-Anon friend of years ago shared in a meeting once that she had to get out of bed each morning, physically get down on her knees and wave a white flag to feel connected to God. I have to pray.

Good Morning Divine Mother, Good Morning Mother Earth, Good Morning all Buddhas, all Enlightened Ones. I surrender; I turn my life, my will over to your care. I pray for the knowledge of your will for me and the power to carry that out.

I offer this prayer of love and compassion, dedicating all of my actions this day to the benefit of all living beings, including me.

I pray today and every day that all my thoughts and words and actions may be divinely led. I pray that I may move forward in confidence knowing that my steps are being guided.

I pray so for these three things: I do surrender totally again; I do turn my life, my will over to your care; I do pray for the knowledge of your will for me and the power to carry that out. I do dedicate all of my actions to the highest good of all beings. I do trust my steps are truly being guided.

I pray for peace, health, a sense of well-being. I thank you for peace, health, a sense of well-being for all beings.

Every day begins with this conversation. Then I review my gratitude list and ask for guidance with anything in particular that is present for me. And then I end the conversation:

Realizing that sentient beings are numberless, I do dedicate all of my actions to the enlightenment of them all. I do release any personal merit I may have gained this life-time toward that end, with total and complete sincerity and joy.

I am so grateful for this daily ritual; so grateful to dedicate this lifetime to service to the highest good of all beings. Pinch me – such a blessing! So grateful!

Candlelight by the sea

It just occurred to me. Yikes! I just picked up one of my favorite rocks carved with the message "*BELIEVE*" as I sit quietly before bed with one candle lit, musing while looking out to the sea from the warmth of my spiritual sanctuary on this cold February evening in La Jolla.

I just looked around to see how many messages you, Divine Mother, have concretely sent to me carved in stone over the last decades. And I am getting it now. One message after another is offering comfort and support and connection which I have been looking for and longing for my entire life.

Tonight my inventory of Your messages all carved permanently in stone –

BELIEVE
MY RELIGION IS KINDNESS
Peace
Thank You
LOVE
TRUST GOD
Nurture
Follow you heart
Blessings
Time heals
Compassion
OM
ShakTi
Hope
Gratitude

All carved in stone; all in my spiritual hermitage by the sea; all part of my life for years and years – and all not connected to my consciousness until this moment somehow.

I am so grateful – always grateful.

I see. You have been with me all along this amazing journey, always adding rocks to my foundation with messages of support; building a foundation that is starting to give me hope of being solid enough to support a new way of being from now on.

Divine Mother

A brilliant spring morning by the sea with the sun streaming in the windows onto me as I sit and write and sit and pray on my meditation cushion…

Divine Mother. The energy is so strong. I have been praying to God and Mother Earth as an energy beam from the heavens to the depths of the earth for years and years. God became Divine Mother this morning. So clear. Divine Mother and Mother Earth now connected and so beautiful in my knowing.

Thank you Divine Mother. Gratitude always…

Total Trust in Divine Mother

As I look at this blank page before I begin to write, I realize that is what my life is now – a completely blank canvas awaiting whatever is next. And I know that I do not want to be the one in charge of creating the canvas.

I surrender. I turn my life, my will, over to your care; I pray for the knowledge of your will for me and the power to carry that out. I offer this prayer of love and compassion, dedicating all of my actions this day to the benefit of all living beings, including me. And I pray today and every day that all my thoughts and words and actions may be divinely led; I pray that I may move forward in confidence knowing that my steps are being guided. I want to be in partnership with you Divine Mother for every aspect of my existence.

And so it is. I am so grateful.

Life in Review

I offered to pick up my dear friend Jack and go to an early dinner after my Tuesday afternoon yoga class and we settled into "Spice n Rice" for a quiet dinner and reconnection.

Then Barbara and David walked in with their friend. Barbara and I worked together at PB Junior High in the 1970s – a life time ago. A scientist, David followed former husband Ken's technical research for years and perhaps still does. We all exclaimed how none of us have changed! Daughter Edith Ann is now the mother of two children aged 8 and 10; she was not married when I last had a conversation with Barbara and David. Life in review began.

Then when I was just about to return to the Thai food in front of me in walked Richard and his former wife, he shuffling along and she obviously in service and bored. He got me away from my former husband but thank you, Divine Mother, I am not with him now. I am so very grateful.

Then in walked John and Rosina, he with a new liver and she after a stroke several years ago, both demonstrating clearly that total transformation is possible. They are living examples.

My life in review. And you are so clearly in charge, Divine Mother. And I am so grateful.

Surrender – again and again

In my meditation and prayer time this morning, I had the realization and integration of a great life learning. Yikes! The intellectual piece had come some time ago – the heart piece came today.

And it caused a reflection of how my daily prayer and meditation began more than 30 years ago at the Westin Hotel in Costa Mesa, California. Funny how that time there was so important; I knew then that it was pivotal at some level.

Continual surrender has been part of my daily prayer routine every day since. I am so grateful! And over the years I have developed a deeper and deeper connection to a power so much greater than me – and I could not function without this connection now.

This morning I had a wonderment about how I got to this place in my life, living as I live, doing the work I do, how it all happened. And then a knowing immediately followed – I have just continued to surrender every day of my life, again and again. My request is simple and the same: *"May I please be your bodhisattva today Divine Mother – may all I do be for the highest good of all beings always?"* And the answer is always affirmative.

In doing my life review, I realized that this sacred time and conversation with Divine Mother each day has indeed kept us connected over decades now. What was an intellectual practice at first has evolved over time to a deep heart-knowing practice. I am not alone. I have not been living this life alone. I am not a random accident. I am deeply connected to Spirit and my steps truly have been guided every step of the way in my commitment to service. I am Divine Mother's bodhisattva.

I am beyond blessed and grateful for my daily practice – one day at a time…

Hospice

I got off the airplane. I left my marriage and business partner and our life together and knew I had to do something for someone who was suffering more than me. The first person who ever showed me love in a way I could understand as a child was my father's business associate. Pat Brown had died of lung cancer. I could never do for her what she had done for me for years; she always said *"Just pass it on."* It was time to do service in her name.

In the depths of my personal agony and confusion when nothing made sense, I found my way to San Diego Hospice. After being there just a brief time, I thought I had found my life purpose.

I trained as a hospice volunteer, spending every Thursday at the inpatient hospital. I loved Thursdays. In one of the biggest personal transition times in my life, I was blessed to be present with those making the ultimate transition. Those Thursdays were a sacred time, a totally present and loving time.

Then I felt drawn to do more. I trained to be a bereavement group facilitator. I wanted to help teenagers as I had long ago as a resource specialist in public schools in support of those with the most challenges. I had a masters degree in education and counseling so it seemed a perfect fit to help bereaved teenagers, a group no one else wanted anything to do with.

Instead, after the training, the Volunteer Coordinator assigned me to the bereavement group for parents who had lost children. I am not a parent – knew little to nothing about parenting children other than my professional education – and certainly had never lost a child to death. What was that assignment all about? Why not the teenagers who no one wanted? All divinely ideal? Facilitating that group twice a month became one of the dearest experiences in my life; those who came to the group healed as I did from very major losses.

Hospice work came naturally to me, always filled with ease and grace. Friends marveled about how I could do it; this reaction surprising me as it was joy for me. I thought I had found my mission, my reason for being after hospicing myself from a former existence. I was preparing my PhD dissertation around my new reason for getting up each day, so excited about a meaningful life.

And then I got fired. What?

The Volunteer Coordinator at San Diego Hospice who would not assign me to the challenging teenagers I wanted to help, who knew I would fail at supporting parents who had lost children, who physically and energetically was my opposite in so many ways, was in fact my boss. My bright light shined on her darkness and she was in charge. One day a future life developing; the next day banished from the grounds of San Diego Hospice. More unimaginable grief and sadness hit me and stopped me from moving from the life I had left to this new life of service I imagined. I thought I had found my true calling – and in an instant it all vanished.

I bereaved myself for months until the first visions of the Foundation for Women began to emerge. Dear Loie, a fellow hospice volunteer, stood by my side in my tremendous grief and disbelief, continually affirming my bright light and what that does to others' dark spots. I am and will forever be grateful to Loie for this affirming. It brought me such comfort at the time and the reminder has served me well over the last many years.

I thought I had found my true life purpose but obviously you had other plans for me, Divine Mother. I am filled with gratitude for all that has happened since hospice work was taken from me. Like Jimmy Stewart in *"A Wonderful Life,"* so much has been created that never would have been if You had not had a bigger and better plan than mine.

So grateful – always.

Divine Message

Cleaning the in-basket on my desk and finding so many notes of inspiration…

Always allow for hope!

Loss is an invitation to change

Disability = different ability

What an apostrophe and a space do to impossible – I'm possible

Disruptions = divine interventions

Joy is not in things, it is in us

There is no coming to consciousness without pain

The best way is always through

Freedom is what you do with what's been done to you

You've got to jump off cliffs all the time and build your wings on the way down

If the only prayer you ever said in your whole life was "thank you" that would suffice

We turn to God for help when our foundations are shaking only to learn that it is God who is shaking them

The other side of every fear is freedom

Normal is not something to aspire to; it's something to get away from

So grateful!

Faith

I have become very reliant upon a quote from the editor of *"Women, Spirituality and Transformative Leadership"*:

Faith is our assurance that there is a Divine plan of infinite love at work even in the most challenging moments, and that we are a part of that plan. Faith gives us the confidence to move ahead with vast visions in the face of enormous odds; it is an invitation to work in active partnership with the Divine in service of a better world.

I love this. And have come to read it daily. It is now part of my email signature. After many years of service through the Foundation for Women, which I birthed in 1997 with the help of dear and special friends, the unimaginable happened at the end of 2012. The FFW became the target of a hostile take-over attempt by a donor. And when that failed, three key women in my life left the Foundation to follow the man who led the take-over. It has now been a long time and I am still dealing with the grief of the betrayals and the uncertainty caused by those who departed.

Years ago I read with great interest Sharon Salzberg's book *"Faith"* as I did not think the Buddhist tradition had a place for faith. Sharon brought it into the conversation. And this special quote is continuing it for me. I am so grateful. I have known since first hearing that I should create something to support and help women that I was merely an instrument, a bodhisattva, in bringing this into being, that there was no "me" or "mine" involved. And so it has been all about service, all about being divinely led, all about being the voice for those whose voices are not being heard.

So if it is not mine to fix, not mine to sustain, not mine to own – what is to become of the present reality? I have turned completely to faith. I am sitting more, listening more, asking for direction more – I am being instead of doing. I am as Pema Chodron expressed in her book *"Being Present with Uncertainty."*

And I am practicing forgiveness. I was accused by our former donor of *"living in a place of optimism called denial."* I have forgiven all and reframed that statement to *"living in a place of optimism called Divine."* Forgiving the three women who I thought had my back has been more challenging, but through faith I have come to realize that all is indeed divinely ideal. I have faith that even in the most challenging moments, the Foundation for Women and our commitment to service is part of that plan.

I am so beyond grateful for faith – sustaining me now…

Ask for Help

I awoke long before dawn on this Sunday morning and stayed curled up in a fetal position under the covers to say my prayers and listen to Divine Mother. I heard *"Ask for Help!"* I replied, *"That is not easy for me. I rarely do it."* *"Ask for Help anyway!"* came back to me.

So I planned an email in my mind, a follow-up message to the members of a special circle of women and a couple of good men who had gathered in support of our work a few days earlier in the week. I opened my computer early on this Sunday which is also not my usual behavior. And before I could begin my message, there was a message from my dear spiritual signpost Verniece:

"Most of the important things in the world have been accomplished by people who have kept on trying when there seemed to be no hope at all."— Dale Carnegie

This along with a special message saying, "*This fits you! xoxoxoxox*"

A wonderful inspiring message! I wrote the email and asked for help.

Then shortly thereafter while walking along the sea, I remembered what dear Sister Joan Chittister, who is such an inspiration to me and the world, had said to me recently: *"Those who have gone before us, given their lives to stretch the world another inch, are the ones who are with us still. We're not alone – and certainly not from one another. My love, Joan"*

So while walking, I started asking for more help from those who have been involved with our special Foundation for Women work and have gone on before me – Aimee and Kim and Stephanie and Lisa and Johna and Jan and Murray… They all were committed to stretching the world another inch and more. And I know they are still committed and helping from where they are now.

Yesterday I ached with deep aloneness. Today I feel so connected because I listened to you Divine Mother and the messages coming from you via others. I am so grateful for your messages and my connection to you – tremendous gratitude always.

Peace

I get it. You Divine Mother have guided my steps every step of the way. You have been standing next to me every moment. You let me make my free will decisions. You helped me clean up after those that did not support my highest good – and expanded those that did support my highest good and the highest good of all beings. I get it – finally.

Fake it until you make it is something I learned in Al-Anon years ago. Just keep believing and trusting. So I have. And it has paid off.

I was part of a special women's retreat entitled "Alchemy" organized by Women of Spirit and Faith as 2013 drew to an end. More than 100 women from all over the USA found their way to a setting near the San Francisco Airport for three days of being in circle with each other – at your invitation Divine Mother/ Mother Earth. We honored you, loved you, appreciated you.

And I finally surrendered totally. *"There is no more struggle,"* I said to dear sister Kathe who held the torch for the gathering with her committed team. Release. And then more. Complete release. Total trust. No more angst. Peace. Joy.

I have been surrendering for more than 35 years now daily – may all I do be for the highest good of all beings, including me. May I be your bodhisattva today and every day.

I am grateful for your patience. It took decades for me to completely trust. I wish it had been sooner. I am beyond blessed to live in trust now.

I have so much gratitude for your love and patience Divine Mother, so much joy in finding gratitude always with your help and guidance. Ω

Personal Note

Since I arrived this lifetime, I have never fit. I changed my vibration very early on trying to fit. I practiced hurry, fix it, make it better behavior for decades trying to fit. I built communities in business and philanthropy trying to fit. All an attempt; I do not fit. Why trying so much to aspire to normal?

As I finish this book, every aspect of my life has changed completely in the last many months. Many betrayals. Many losses. Many changes. Many people gone. Every aspect – relationships, lifestyle, work – all changed completely; everything except my connection to my spiritual signpost and teacher Verniece and to you Spirit.

I am holding your hand Divine Mother, living in complete trust, taking the next indicated step; choosing love instead of fear; total surrender. And I have a deep knowing – I don't need to know. I have been trying to figure it out, make sense of this adventure, trying to fit my entire life. Now instead I am in complete trust. I don't need to know. And I finally know that I am not alone.

As my dear friend Maria says, *"This is so fabulous! Complete transformation is happening in every aspect of your life!"*

And from dear friend Laurie – *"For a seed to achieve its greatest expression, it must come completely undone. The shell cracks, its insides come out and everything changes. To someone who doesn't understand growth, it would look like complete destruction."* Cynthia Occelli

And finally this from Sufi poet Hafiz –

The Seed Cracked Open

It used to be
That when I would wake in the morning
I could with confidence say,
"What am "I" going to
Do?"

That was before the seed
Cracked open.

Now Hafiz is certain:

There are two of us housed
In this body.

Doing the shopping together in the market and
Tickling each other
While fixing the evening's food.

Now when I awake
All the internal instruments play the same music:

"God, what love-mischief can "We" do
For the world
Today?"

GRATITUDE Always…

Made in the USA
Charleston, SC
08 December 2014